for Don Metz and Peter Woerner, with love,

& in recollection of some of life's best rambles

a little wildness:

Story Line Press

some notes on rambling

Sydney Lea

ISBN: 1-58654-046-7

Library of Congress Catalog Number pending

A paperback original

Story Line Press, Inc.

Three Oaks Farm

P.O. Box 1240

Ashland, OR 97520-0055

www.storylinepress.com

Art & design of book & cover by Jane Ransom

contents

prelude

THANKS PROBABLY TO GENES AND CERTAINLY TO PRACTICE, I've got a good bump of location (as the older Yankees still call it hereabouts); it's pretty hard to cross me up in the northeastern forest. Still, I'll now and then recognize that I've been bushwhacking for some time at a slightly or even a radically different angle from what I imagined.

That's usually a good turn of events. It may in fact be what the following book is "about." It's certainly what that book will somehow do.

On such occasions, I'll burst out of the puckerbrush, my face festooned with spiderwork in the warm months, my snowshoes a chaos of pine-whiskered iceballs in the cold. When that happens, I'll find myself....

Yes, I'll find myself. It's a strange thing, but even if the rambler and the writer should seek to avoid all double entendre, and not just that afforded by language, to get at the actual in its fullest actuality, that effort is inevitably thwarted. Stranger still, it's from such defeat of intention that we arrive at our fulfillments. One thinks of the Christian teaching that the new man cannot come to life unless the old one die.

Complex stuff, to say it far too mildly. More about it as I travel.

What I'd meant to say was, I'll suddenly find myself looking down or up or out on territory familiar as my thumb, but looking from so unfamiliar a perspective that I'm temporarily convinced of something strange and certainly wrong: Life starts all over from now.

Better a false sense of rebirth than none at all. Or so I always claim—especially if such delicious fantasy can go on repeating itself, as it has done for me, and does, and I pray will do.

For I am a rambler, or I am nothing at all.

Am I just delusional? Maybe yes, maybe no, probably both. We'll see about that too as we go through a dark wood or many; or a bright one or many; or anywhere we roam, come to think of it. Rambling is rather a matter of lost and found, as I've implied; but I mustn't get ahead of myself: I'll be doing enough of that in what follows.

As I leave the indoors behind here, it seems fitting for me to recall a specific moment from many years ago, one lively as ever in mind. I've gone up a certain favorite mountain, off-trail. Along the freshets, the trout lilies gather in their huddles. Climbing, wandering, I've sniffed out not only the more common red but also the painted trillium beds amid the north slope wetland. I've reflected on the odd concatenation of the flowers' fetid odor, their beauty, their fragility, their hiddenness; I've vaguely imagined them as emblems, found in them a not quite mute commentary on life itself, human and natural.

For the rambler, each sense will in his more elevated (or depressed) moments inform the other, so that each flower has reeked just now both of mortal splendor and splendid mortality and all their manifestations, bodily and spiritual. Each is as fresh and new as it is old and memory-laced. Senses interfuse, but so do memories and anticipations, bygones and presents and hopes and fears.

A self is a thing both fluid and habit-bound, just as wildness is a thing both rife with permanences and ever-changing.

In any case, I stand in this memory at the mountain's rounded summit, a sort of granite dune. The wind is now bossy, now mild, now gone, now creeping or blundering in from a different quarter. Around me the conifers upthrust themselves, knee-high, which is to say as high as they'll ever get, not because I'm above timberline—I'm not—but because, as the farmers whose scions now live amid the rich, black soil of the Midwest so quickly and shockingly discovered, vegetation's roots don't go very deep in this country before they run against the sort of stone on which I rest here.

Combine a shallow top layer of earth with four- or five-month winters, and you have something to marvel at and maybe mope about: it's a wonder, all things considered, that I've ever seen even the shyest bloom, that these cabbagey firs and spruces still bother to thrive at all, in any form. Corn snow still dots this lofty ground, though it's late April, and those pitiable shocks of greenery start something rolling in my head—something about valor and endurance, about what, though this is no place for a Frenchman, the aphoristic French call *l'élan vital.* In any case, start something they do, because they've done so all my life.

There's an old song about coal miners. It claims that going deep into the earth will "form as a habit and seep in your soul." No miner, I, but I do understand that concept of seepage: rambling, though it may appear counter-habitual by its nature, has subtly possessed me over the years, so that I simply cannot imagine a life without it.

So I catch myself on the familiar and risky point of allegorizing as I look down, or, risky too, I look up. The sun's as dim as pewter, and the mare's tails crawl across it, now and then magically, instantly puffing, fattening: it's spring, and it's winter, it's windy and not.

And Lord, how short is a life.

And Lord, how devoid of novelty, such a reflection! Its very banality galls, because like every rambler, I persistently ask the question posed by New England's own Ralph Emerson, puzzling, potent: Why should we not enjoy an original relation with Nature?

As if in self-defense, like one who forces eyes open against nightmare, I look down again. Farther out this time, much farther. Something original may lie there, something actually new. One never knows.

I look over yonder, and what do I see? Miles below my granite heap, on a patch of pale spring grass, I spot a dash of white. It's a dog, I surmise, though I can't be sure of that. It could as easily be a towel left drying in the sunshine, a newspaper left behind by some loller who's gone back into the kitchen for another cup of coffee, a child's tricycle. Truth is, I can't even really make out the color itself: that angel white could in fact be yellow, the yellow could be roan, because the sun's not pewter at all for an instant, then it is again, then not, and the subservient world and its hues must scrabble to heed these changes.

But the mind will have its way—always, it seems. And so, on no ground whatsoever except the ground I stand upon and the way it somehow breathes into me, I abruptly assure myself of particulars: I'm indeed observing a dog, and not just any dog but some breed of hound.

Next I make her a bitch, then I make her old, and I put her harrying years well behind her. After all, an unpenned hound in its prime usually means a hound in the woods, not one flopped in a dooryard. I instantly feel respect for the animal's own valor, her endurance, the way she ragged all those big-going, long-winded white hares through her working years, running them often till the flat-topped moon jumped up over this very mountain and the night birds came out to whoop and in the lunar light she could see bright crystals strung on air. Now she nears the end of a life that's been full; great satisfaction in the fullness; but now it's ending.

Her four feet twitch in dream: the buck hare has just cleared that little tussock ahead and is back into the black swamp on the clean jump. But surely she's gaining. She whines, as close as she can get in her sleep to a full cry.

I think of my own fellow houndsman, Allie Pike, home again, recovering nicely from his mild coronary; if I know the man, we'll be ragging the hare again come late fall, together, his young male hound's big voice filling those woods down there, and there, and there.

Is that a kennel a few yards beyond my hound? I make it so; and, inside its chainlink, two further squibs of color, which must be two other dogs at rest, lazing on sun-warmed concrete. Let them be lithe, I say, and lithe they are. Bird dogs? Whose?

A yellow house nearby. That much is no fancy.

Dogs. Kennel. House. Blue truck in a driveway. Pretty meadow climbing the sidehill, stopped short by a rockfence, second growth beyond. Clapboard bowing away from an unpainted woodshed. (Imagination again.) Swing for a child, tractor tire strung to a treelimb. (Likewise.) Mailbox canting toward a roadside ditch (likewise again), as if to illustrate the old, half-accurate saw about no news being good news.

Yet this, I now see in a flash, is no mere imaginative construct. What I observe, with inward and outward eye alike, is something I've observed at valley level, again and again and again.

All that is—mine.

Mine. From so distant and unanticipated a perspective it takes longer than you'd expect for me to recognize this frail claim to possession: then all at once it's as if these familiars were uncannily rearranged. For one thing, of course, I can see them now, so to speak: yes, a hound—beagle, female; yes, two pointers—females as well; yes, a locust tree, a hanging tire, a Ford truck, an open-mouthed and dented mailbox, so on.

Something has seeped in my soul.

All at once too, in this rearrangement these beings and objects become eloquent of things that have passed in their neighborhood—things big and small that pass there now and that will later pass, things I've never pondered in quite the same way before.

The next cloud, suddenly just there, is immense; the sky goes cobalt, and instantly I feel the spirit chill. There is an aloneness in me. There is, I know, in anyone. Yet why should I actively seek it, even cultivate it, only at times like this to be made unhappy by it, if "unhappy" is even halfway suitable a term? What has convinced me that I need that zero solitude if I have any hope of overcoming it? Why do I claim to want its overcoming at all? For chill is only the half of what's going on in me.

Whatever I feel on this dear mountain, it can't simply be a matter of topography. Southward of that yard down there, on any map, psychic or actual, Trout Brook's falls still purl, bright and puny, hidden by greengrowth a few hundred yards in from Mort Bailey's gravel pit. My oldest son and I once spied a mink there, caught him as he plucked a nuthatch from its inverted grasp on a hemlock trunk. We watched the tiny predator coming, keeping on the blind side of the tree; we saw him skirt the trunk at last in a dazzling rush, picking off the bird as a cat does a butterfly.

There are a lot of people, I remember thinking, who don't know that mink eat birds at all; I was glad to be one who did. I'd seen the kill, not just read of it: peach breastfeathers exploding into the thawing March breeze, headshake of the doughty dark weasel, pink-red glyphs of blood on snow.

That afternoon I was not on a ramble, no, but rather in the heated cab of my truck; and I was in company, beloved company, even if my boychild was so young (four? five?) that he found the moment far less wondrous than I, and today may not remember it at all.

No, I wasn't rambling. I was not even alone, as the rambler somehow needs to be. But the incident made me think of heading out solo, just to see, like the bear who crossed to his mountain's other side, what I could see. And so I soon did, and did again, and do, and will do forever and ever amen.

No, not topographical, all this. The woodpecker-savaged butternut still marks the spot near the pit where you'd swing into the growth if you wanted to find the Baileys' falls, or even better, hear them; the tree's still losing limbs to bird and bug and every other opportunist—it'll be gone in much less than my lifetime. The suicide timber baron, Fred Wagner, once had a barn across the dirt road; the structure's moldered now to nothing, and remembers itself only by making a darkness on the small remnant of field before it, ancient manure-dust still hot enough to melt a rectangle into the shallow snow. Milkweed and hardhack will soon clamber skyward there, life going on.

From here, from now, everything I survey—animate and inanimate—is for a moment newly framed, no matter what its condition. I've been shocked into contemplation by an odd arrival at an odd lookout, and for some reason that makes me more able than usual to evaluate the frame's contents.

But how to say what I mean?

I turn and race downhill, almost falling with every step, a young and aging and daunted and joyous man.

(anti-)definitions

IT BEGINS WITH AN ITCH.

But more on that later. For now, since I mean to write at some length about rambling, I should first define the term, even if definition's often the rambler's enemy, an object of assault.

Assault? No. Too angry.

I can start describing a ramble by way of what it's not. To begin with, it's hardly grand scale stuff: the area I cover in the foot travels I mention hereafter can't amount to much more than a few hundred acres of forest, ledge and hillside. Surprising, delightful, how many fresh explorations and discoveries I can make in such small ranging.

There's the way in late winter, at a certain spot to my northwest, halfway up John Renfrew's ridge, snow will come sideways through a granite gap if the wind's blowing up from the Connecticut River. It will, that is, come *uphill*, while all around the flakes fall straight as a die. Sometimes I can peek over a steep ledge in the exact opposite quarter, southeast, where the jackfirs grow so thick you have to crawl through them; but the deer themselves, does and skippers mostly, manage somehow to navigate that doghair. They make the greenery vibrate with their subtle passings: to see this is almost like watching a breeze shake a thicket of late cornstalks, but for the snap glimpse of hoof or hock.

And the ravens are their own variety and plenitude: some blare, some coo, some gawp, some chuckle, some bray; one bird fighting a high wind is the very figure of loneliness, a flock in the trees above some winterkill an illustration of *crowd*.

One summer, for reasons no expert could explain to me, the grass snakes bloomed; in every cleared spot or old burn you'd find not two or three but 20, lolling in the dust or inscribing it with their going.

And the vernal pools are full of grayfrogs and wood ducks and newts.

Along the ridge we call The Lookout, the in-line tracks in snow or mud of a red fox, and now and then the quick animal itself, here and in the instant gone, his bush the one that Durer caught perfectly in that great print.

The busy-ness of cat tracks around The Lookout's ledges, the *thoroughness* of their hunting!

So many signs and so many landscapes within the one I frequent, yes. But as you hear me, it's still clear I'm not talking about technical climbing, big time orienteering, the Iditarod, spelunking, or anything of the kind. What I do rarely means risky physical business, although it can turn into that—unexpectedly.

The rambler does find thrills, even sublime ones, but usually and necessarily does so more or less by accident.

"Accident": the noun's derived from a combination of Latin words that suggest "a falling toward," and given my belief that words contain their own histories even as usage changes, in this case a ghostly meaning reveals something crucial about the literary bushwhack I'm headed for.

When ramblers set out, they abandon any aim beyond the ramble itself; map, compass, any instrument of precision stays home. This is crucial, definitive. We actually *want* to fall (or blunder or grope or feel our way) towards our fulfillments; we can't just march right at them, plot them. If we do that we're not rambling at all.

Will power plays a part in all this, but only in so far as it kicks itself out of the picture, allowing other dimensions of mind to work freely—which is to say, at the risk of raising eyebrows, that there's a meditative aspect of the pursuit. That trillium invokes it, or that blur of a distant dog's white parts and its opening of the mind's eye; that mink-memory; that puff of nuthatch feather and down. On and on.

What I've already ruled out makes it almost unnecessary to cite other inadmissibles: those Global Positioning Systems, for example, satellite-aided, hand-held devices which you see nowadays in outdoor catalogs, and which invite any out-of-shape oaf into the wild, promising he won't get lost. He can press a button or two, and be led by his "virtual" hand back to where he started or wherever else he wants to go, including the nearest McDonald's, I guess.

We seek not that virtuality but rather physicality. We will defend the physical to our dying days—in part because, without it, we have no access to the spiritual. That paradox is at the center of our beings and doings, at the center of this book.

Such contraptions as the GPS run against the grain of a rambling passion, whose "virtues" are almost exactly opposite from the machine's. After all, the fellow with the GPS might just as well, in a rambler's view, bring a television into any version of wildness; in fact he already does. But such behavior really makes little difference in his case, because he was barred long ago from the richer moments I want to consider. If he weren't, he'd never have bought his little system in the first place. The same applies to anyone who feels a desperate need to plug in when he's out: e-mail, walkie-talkie, cellular phone, camcorder, what have you?

No matter where he may be, even in backcountry, such a person is the Anti-Rambler: rather than going to wildness as an escape from the busy world of purpose and its encumbering tools, he brings that mess along for the outing. He's too full of purpose.

This is scarcely to say that ramblers' ventures *lack* purpose altogether; we naturally expect rewards from what we do. It's just that our pay-offs, like our itineraries, can't be predetermined. What we hunt is not specifiable, calculable, calibrated; our ends—spiritual, geographical, physical—don't live there.

My effort at definition is evaporating before I've even really cleared my throat. And yet I'll go on clearing it for a moment, because I share the contrariness of any rambler, and am therefore frequently inclined to counter-example rather than example. If I've been talking about what we don't do, then, now I'll talk about *where* we don't do it, can't.

If homesickness were an odd condition, it might be odd to begin these meditations not in my beloved upper New England but in the Ticino, Italian Switzerland, whose benign and well upholstered bosom will cradle our family for the next six months. I'm teaching at a local college, our children attend local schools, my wife is on a well deserved professional sabbatical.

There are plenty of reasons *not* to be homesick. Nobel laureate Hermann Hesse must have known as much when he came here: in our Swiss town of Montagnola, he composed some of his major works, which my generation once considered sublime thrills in their own right. The village center boasts a Hesse museum, in fact. Forty years ago, proto-Aquarian kids like me would have swarmed the place; this morning, its custodian seemed almost shocked when I showed up to look around. Of course she was polite and patient, even more so than the average Ticino native. In other words, damned near to a fault.

I liked several of Hesse's small oil paintings, liked them more at least than I now like his novels. For an author, a cautionary note may lurk in that. But I'll try to ignore such heavy stuff in what follows, if only because I, or any writer, must after all keep rambling ahead or else wither; that's about our only choice, it seems to me, or at least it's mine. I lately learned, for example, that I missed this year's literary-American brass ring, was not the winner but one of three finalists for the Pulitzer Prize in poetry. What to do about that? Curse and mope? No, keep rambling.

From our rented house, we can see Lake Lugano in the relatively near distance, the whited Alps in the far. In our yard, snow bends the palm-fronds, which is completely exotic and marvelous to us, whose permanent home lies in Vermont. (I think obliquely of brown pelicans in the Yellowstone Valley.)

That view can rob your breath, no two ways about it. But having considered it at all hours, I recognize that it's—well, it's just different. If rambling requires elevation, and it does, it's not the sort I can see all around us now.

The same goes for density, a still greater requirement. The local prospects just seem too wide—and too easy to come by. We ramblers do want prospects, but as I've already suggested we want somehow to happen, or even stumble or fall upon them. Vistas can't be there for any old eye; you can't just pluck them, so to speak, like the hazelnuts in our Swiss backyard; they can't be accessible from the get-go; they have to reveal themselves suddenly—and briefly: a few steps' worth at a time.

As our Yankee predecessors might have said, we need to feel we've *earned* our perspectives. That's just in our characters.

Character

Does all this mean that ramblers are Yankee "Puritans"?

Not necessarily. By my lights rambling does seem a largely Appalachian game, but not exclusively New English: it's as entirely available in more southerly parts of the range, clear down to Georgia, as in northern Maine, New Hampshire or Vermont. And who'd deny that there's more evidence of striving—which, even thinking in secular terms, we might link to the Pilgrim notion of manifest "saintliness" or election—in a climb up one of the Rockies than up one of our own time-gnawed hills? The same's true of all the so-called high-adventure enterprises I mentioned above, and in all parts of the world.

Scarlet Letter-style guilt plays no role, either, in what we ramblers do, at least not so far as I can see just now. (Who knows? I may blunder into some reason to change my mind about that and many another thing in these pages.)

I won't really get much past vague generality, you see, no matter how many words I spend nor how many examples I think of: if you need something crisper, then, you could try asking some other rambling characters about this issue of character. I should warn, however, that in spite of my own extensive and ongoing experience, I've only known a few true ramblers at all, and fewer still who could or would honor your question: Annie Fitch; David Tobey; Earl Bonness; Landy Bartlett; Annie Proulx; Joey Olsen; Peter Woerner; Ray Hulett; Don Metz; a scattering of others. And even if it sounds presumptuous of me, I bet they'll be just as nonspecific as I am.

Hail, however (or therefore), to each and all, and in a case or two, farewell.

Decades ago, in my position today, some of these friends might have said, "The hell with rambling anyhow." (I know I would have, though I'm far from bragging on that account.) They'd have looked around at the *human* scenery in this corner of the world and then attempted other peaks, as it were.

My current students and the Ticinesi in general are among the most beautiful men and women I've ever seen. It seems strange, then, even to me, that although I like many of these people, some almost enormously, I don't register lust for a one.

This isn't just because I'm more happily married than anybody deserves. It's something else. Surely I'm not Puritanical, so maybe I'm simply old-fashioned. Or maybe, like most of my rambler chums by now, I'm a bit old, period. Because I know that the local lovelies' physical attributes would once have blinded me to any of their defects, if that's what they are; I wouldn't have been put off, for instance, to see that like all well-heeled and even modest western Europeans in our time these locals are if anything more fetishistic about goods and commodities than North Americans. In a recent issue of *La Repubblica*, for instance, I read that 79% of Italian teens own a wireless phone, and I'd be shocked if young Swiss weren't more than up to speed on that score.

I thought of this statistic during a break between classes yesterday morning, when I looked out my office window at a girl (forgive me: she's that) who could easily be taken for a model from one of the haute couture outfits in nearby Milan. She sipped her *macchiato* with one hand, the other hand seemingly grafted to her stylish and skinny *telefonino*, into whose mouthpiece she breathed....

Well, I was about to say she breathed inanities, but how could I of all people hop to such a damning assumption? I turned back to my desk with a private grimace, suddenly wondering what the New Haven citizenry thought about me circa 1960: Yale freshman, both smalltown provincial and pretentious, all decked out and ludicrous—spanking ascot, tasselled loafers, the whole bit. Did my act appear any less witless than the one I'd just observed from my office window? Did it inspire someone's disgust, even a moderate version like mine as I studied the pretty girl and her cell phone and ankle-length leather overcoat and five-inch block heels, which made her totter on the flagstone but here appear to be absolutely *de rigueur?*

Memory of my own younger years ought to check my disgust, all right—and my instinct to criticize. Old scout that I've become, though, I felt troubled late on an Alpine morning, the sun like clear-day Colorado's, the snowy ring of mountains lit like flares, that our beautiful youngster's eyes showed a dismaying blankness. Or was it just that she focused, hard, on whatever she was saying and hearing over the airwaves?

Yes, who was I to judge? Still, I'd have had more faith in the importance of those telephonic mutterings, exclamations, moans and giggles if at the end of one conversation she hadn't, with her glossy talons, immediately punched up a next. And then a next and next and next without interruption, as if a simple moment of simple breath struck simple dread in her simple soul.

If you weren't so much older, you might want a young woman like that, and never mind what seems like shallowness; but you don't now, do you? For my part, anyhow, I really and only wanted to tell her about that discomfort of mine—as if telling her about it, or about anything, were my business. As if I could know what the good life should be for her generation or another.

Hell, I don't even speak with any confidence about what a "generation" ever meant (the canard about the "boring" but "placid" '50s of my own adolescence now striking me as so much horseshit, just for example). I can speak with even less authority about the meaning of "goodness."

Old fart, heal thyself. So I said in silence, then went back to where I am now.

Ramble as poem

AND YET LET ME TALK ABOUT SOMETHING GOOD, SOMETHING VERY GOOD, which can turn up on a ramble, and in my experience frequently does. I can testify to it in part because I'm a member of a generation *senza* cell phone (or television or Walkman or video game), or at least of the generation's luckier portion by my reckoning. That evaluation, of course, may put me in the timeless category of aging folks who imagine the barbarism of the young, which is always imagined to be world-ending too, and which somehow never is.

At least I know my own banality.

In the following book it doesn't overly matter if you like poetry, dislike it, or like most don't think about it much one way or the other. So no one has a thing to worry about on that score, even if I'll be quoting from poems now and then. You can't stop me from doing that; the habit figures into whatever I am.

For example, there's a passage from T. S. Eliot's "Little Gidding" that connects, as I take it anyhow, with what I spoke of in my prelude:

> *We shall not cease from exploration*
> *And the end of all our exploring*
> *Will be to arrive where we started*
> *And know the place for the first time.*

T. S. Eliot? Just hear me, parrotting that oh-so-urbane, Olympian poet, the last writer in history who'd ever have led or followed me on what I'm calling a ramble! He's also one, frankly, I don't give much of a damn about, hardly ever going back to his work, at least not to later poems like that one.

Yet I'm not much troubled by this or by any other apparent contradiction in my ramble, partly because consistency (Emerson's "hobgoblin of little minds") is one of the traps, like definition, that I'm skirting as a rambler. Nor does such poetizing conflict with my outdoorsy persona, because I don't for one minute present myself as some Natty Bumppo or noble savage or even as a real countryman in any sense that the friendliest of my neighbors would accept. As one of them brilliantly put it to me many years back, I've never "pulled tits at five o'clock in January." Amen.

Meaning what? That the contradictions I embody limit my authorial authority here? Hell, it's limited anywhere. Like any author's. Like anyone's.

What *am* I, then? A rambler, sure enough, but also a somewhat more than commonly literate person, fancily educated, on paper anyhow, complete with Ivy League Ph.D. And I'm a poet myself, a fact whereby I'll try to excuse further oceans of inconsistency in what's coming—I've always suspected, you see, that *any* poet (even the self-described "Classicist, Catholic, Monarchist" St. Louis kid, T. S. Eliot) has to be at least part rambler. And as I've already said, ramblers aren't apt to know when they set out where they'll end up, nor how, and they're apt to be happy about that, discovery being, after all, one of the rambler's truly principal pleasures. The predetermined, well marked trail: well, that's not the path to his delight or enlightenment.

And that's what makes ramblers "poetic," if you'll pardon the term. A poet would find no point in recording what he or she knew before the writing even began—unless his or her taste lay in scholarship or reportage or opinion, all of which, I assume from my distance, provide their own rewards for some people, just as non-rambling travel through the outdoors provides it for others.

I may be charged with speaking for small minorities, and no one knows the justice of that charge better than I do. I speak for poets or ramblers or, even rarer, maybe hens-tooth rare, for rambling poets and poetic ramblers. In any case, whether they've ever written a strophe or not, I hope to address any and all who like me insist that the richest satisfactions lurk in unscripted outings, over the landscape, over the page.

Or both.

Or perhaps even over life.

Maybe, of course, though I hope not, I speak for no one but myself, whom I've sometimes described as a man in the woods with his head full of books, and a man in books with his head full of the woods. One role keeps checking the other, definition fights definition, one label resists another, one sense of precision invites a different sense—and on I wander.

Those tensions, I confess, tempt me just to give up on definition/label/precision altogether, which, if I understand my own psychic dynamics, would mean giving up any pretense to consecutive "story" in the bargain. I can't really help any of that: I have to digress now and then, just as I have to sneeze. On the other hand, I may digress into story itself.

Or anecdote anyhow:

Allie Pike, an officer and a houndsman

He was the road commissioner (the best I've known in any north-country town) for the first village to call me its citizen; that is, the first to let me vote, for Allie or anyone. Thirty-odd years ago.

Allie and I started to know each other by listening to our dogs plowing the Grafton County sidehills and swamps after "snowshoe rabbits" (or more properly, varying hare). Blended music, always. His dog was tall, mixed beagle and foxhound, a good one for deep snow; and he was, as they say, ball-mouthed, his voice coming low, ominous, drawn-out, whatever the stage of the run; it belonged, I'd joke, in a horror movie. Mine was pure 15-inch beagle, Penny Tune, and whether she was just started or in full chase, she always sounded as jaunty as her name: chop-chop-yip.

With the years, Allie and I came to know each other in a lot of different ways than as fellow houndsmen, though I don't think we would have done so without those hounds, those rabbits, that snow-cover, that music. The bonds formed by hunters are at best ridiculed, at worst attacked, in our time; but that doesn't keep them from being genuine—especially when there's a dog or two in the mix.

Now I don't care a thing about eating a snowshoe hare, and didn't then. I ate more than my share of them, simply because I don't shoot what I don't put on my table. In Penny's waning years, I much more often than not just let her run, no kill on my mind; I'd shoot a rabbit every now and then, yes, but only by way of rewarding her valor. She did love to prance about with an animal almost as long as she was in her mouth, shaking it terrier-like, the blood spraying into the puckerbrush, Allie's hound chasing her for a taste of his own.

I cooked my game in as many ways as I knew how. Annie Proulx gave me some Moroccan recipe of all things (varying hare in north Africa?), and that made it a pretty decent feed. Still it was a labor: you didn't just fire up the stove, as you would with a wild duck or a grouse, and have a delectable meal in less than half an hour. Not that snowshoes were repulsive; they just weren't especially toothsome.

It's another sort of taste I retain from all those hunts in any case, now that I've quit chasing the hare and have no hound of any kind. It's standing there with Allie, both our heads cocked to a distant, blended melody; it's sharing our own imagined narrative of what's going on there on the little mountain behind Mud Turtle Pond. It's hearing ice buckle on the pond itself, and the first barred owls beginning to chant back and forth at one another, with the first of moonlight showing up behind the knoll, and the Saint Johnsbury-bound freight train whistling low from crossriver. It's smelling the cold of the coming night, just as on other nights you can smell snow in the making, before a flake has dropped.

It's being in the right company at the right time in the right place. Which is to say that it's not rambling, though it's something wonderful enough on its own.

Rambling. I'm pretty sure it was Allie who came up with the term, which I'm so clumsily trying to define. It was once when he caught me as I broke out of the woods below the hare ground that (for forgotten but doubtless resonant reasons) we called The Hedgehog Den. He sat high on his grader, with which he'd been cuffing the early frost heaves from Whipple Hill Road. Although the game was still in season, there I stood, all gun- and dogless. I was—what? Oddly embarrassed? A bit, I puffily imagined, like naked, sinful Adam in the Garden.

I knew he'd ask me what I'd been up to, and, over the rumble of diesel, he did. I couldn't quite specify my intentions for Allie, any more than I'm doing for you. Instead I told him about a thing or two I'd seen up near The Den: not just the maze of rabbits' beats we already well knew of, but other things, like the tracks of a restless bear, who should still have been in quasi-hibernation.

"By the Jesus, somethin'll move them all the same now and then," said Allie; he had a rapid-fire delivery, spat out his sentences, almost as if he were angry. "Had little ones, likely. Sow bear."

The black bear throws her one or two young in February, often without knowing she's done so, because they're only gopher-sized and she's at least drowsy. The newborns simply make their way to the snoozing mother's teat and hang on till it's time to do something else.

Allie clipped right along: "Even if it wa'n't cubs, somethin'll give her the itch, seems like." He stomped his clutch and reached for his shift lever. "Guess she wanted a little ramble," he said. Then, with a final, puzzled look down at me, he added: "Guess you wanted one too, Mister Man."

Guess by the Jesus I did, I do.

Some other good things that can show up on a ramble

A SCARLET TANAGER IN AUGUST, OUT OF HIS DEEP WOODS, CLOSE TO DIRT road: not far in fact from Allie's pig hovel, where I also saw an indigo bunting once, same time of year. I've seen many others, but those birds stopped me in my tracks, both mental and psychic.

The bitch coyote—not especially handsome, mutt-brindly in fact—standing broadside for what seem minutes (more likely seconds), the wind against her and with me; I could see it lift her guard hairs, she was that nearby, then she moved up the May freshet, snuffing at every depression in its tiny bank, pawing at some.

Ten yards from where I rested on a rock, a cock ruffed grouse drumming on a fallen softwood, which nobody ever sees him do except in photographs taken by people who devote a life....

A wild June columbine stalk with good flower, unlikely as hell in such ground, I'd have thought, where the blueberry and groundpine clotted the ledgy soil; how had this rugged little shock of magenta made its way? Who knows? Not me; it just had.

Similarly, asters, Philadelphia fleabane, managing to survive among much taller marsh grasses down in that wetland below Bruce and Leslie's. September.

A fisher who, when I startled him, treed and skipped off through the canopy as quickly as a man might change his mind; he was just now there, though! And so was I, even more remarkable.

I dream in each of these many moments (as often as I've dreamed otherwise) that beauty will prevail after all.

And some even more inexplicable phenomena, mostly of human origin: what in hell was the story behind that old-fashioned kapok-filled life vest, hung in a tree on Piper's Ridge, miles from any water deep enough to let you take a drink standing up, 1000 feet above sea-level? Or that high-heeled slipper in a cleft of sheer granite wall near my turkey grounds, no trail worth its name within a half-hour's hike?

It all makes a fellow think, I can never help saying, too stunned to resist the ready cliché.

A brief inventory of stuff

WHAT STUFF DO YOU NEED FOR RAMBLING? WELL, ABOVE ALL YOU NEED that itch, an almost physical irritation, which tells you something, however hazy, about a little wildness in your soul and how it chimes with a little wildness Out There.

Of course, there are all kinds of itches among humankind, all kinds of prompts to thought or action or both: I have a broker friend, for instance, who ever since his earliest adulthood has squirmed on his mattress before daylight, aching to get to the office, his head charged full of daydreams about what the market will do before he gets back into the same bed. Most of his contemporaries have retired; but he's still at it, lying there with his visions.

Not for me, that particular life and that manner of vision, though I like and admire this broker very much. I only mention him to acknowledge the part of the itch in all men and women who savor their lives far more often than they regret them. At least that's true among the ones I've known. You can follow some extrinsic agenda while you're young, it seems. I did. You can still be more or less content with that. But there comes a day.

Apart from the itch, not much equipment is really necessary for a rambler: a pair of feet in reasonable shape, a serviceable set of muscles and joints. And even if these get a bit iffy, rambling's not out of the question. It's like what they say about golf (of all hideous thoughts!): you can do it long as you can move.

One thing's certain: ramblers aren't gear people, and may indeed be *contras* in that regard. For us, there's no point in thumbing through the glossy Orvis catalog for stuff. Rambling isn't suited to anyone's fatuous desire to be a gentleman on some supposed British model, so badly suited anyhow to our kind of wildness. Rambling, in fact, is to Orvis's style as the thing itself is to the thing commodified.

But why pick on Orvis, which is hardly our chief villain, maybe not even a particularly notable one? No, ours isn't the domain of the would-be Old World gent; but it's not that of the hook-and-bullet-and-loudness types either, with their fish- and depth-finders, jet skis, downriggers, 150-horse Mercs, ORVs, SUVs.

The twain, of course, at some point meets, precisely when we arrive at exploitation's border. Orvis's marketing strategy makes me wince, even shudder. So does L. L. Bean's, whose mail-order offerings nowadays must send poor old Leon Leonwood, the company's founder—whom I was lucky enough to bump into once on a landlocked salmon stream—to snap-rolling in his grave.

But even if the obsession with gear, with stuff, differs in nuance for the hook-and-bullet folks, who have no pseudo-aristocratic intentions whatever, it really shows the same impulses under the surface. I also wince, for example, when I bump into that guy in the drift boat who, each time he hooks a fish, punches his cell phone to inform some pal in Houston of the "line-stretcher" he's into. His guide studies the shore, non-plussed.

That man casts a nice bug. (I'm watching him despite myself.) He knows what he's doing when it comes to fooling and playing a big trout. He's probably a more proficient fly angler than I am, I admit. But if I talked to him about rambling, I suspect he'd look at me as if I were a bug myself.

At the landing downstream, our line-stretcher specialist will get into his Lincoln Navigator. It has an NRA sticker in its back window, a computer to give him highway directions in the dash. He's been using an Orvis rod.

The twain.

Rambling splits that twain, I hope.

What the hell does that mean, to split a twain? I can hardly tell: it's as if the words there took over, God bless and damn them both. I only mean that rambling rejects either of the dreary options I've just sketched. That's because rambling attaches itself primarily to—the primary. It rejects the notion that the right stuff will help us much, that it has anything to do with providing spiritual results.

I know I repeat myself, for emphasis, when I say that rambling wants a pause from immersion in the commercialized, wired, gadgety world, irresistible as that world is, no matter how I or anyone may try to interfere with it. Rambling wants out of the realm of cell phone towers, which spring into being, even up where my family lives, faster than second growth woods; on clear nights, you see the higher ones twinkling from what were boondockiest New England hills not long ago. It wants out of voice mail and Fax. Out.

Rambling also turns from the related world of those so-called outfitters who announce—in each last ad you'll see in each last magazine from *Guns*

& Ammo to *Gray's Sporting Journal* or on their damnable websites—that their facilities are "suitable for corporate functions." Cast in the morning, network at noon, blast in the p.m., take a meeting after supper.

Spread-sheets and safaris? Royal Coachmen and royalties? Is that what it's come to? Yes, I'm afraid. But ramblers will go down rambling, Mister Man. No matter if he and she have never so much as wet a line or pulled a trigger, intuition will tell them that to transfer the experience of a fish, a gamebird, a deer to the airwaves, to the Internet or whatever, is never to have experienced the creature in the first place. Photocopying a trout or grouse into those outfitters' slick advertisements or tacking their feeble likenesses onto the company bulletin board? Ditto.

Go to hell, you.

A wild being should remain an essence, a wonder, *ding an sich*, not a commodity of any sort. We're talking of two different worlds here, though making that kind of distinction's getting to be a harder and harder business.

True confessions

DID I JUST SAY "BUSINESS"? EVEN MY RIGHTEOUS INDIGNATION BORROWS the vocabulary it wants to kick out, at least out of locales where the vocabulary, and all it implies, doesn't belong.

Furthermore, despite all my mourning for the vanishing primary world, I'm as compromised as the next man. Am I depressed to see man-tracks, for instance, in the Hedgehog Den or in any backcountry spot where they never used to be? Of course. The planet has gotten too crowded, I mutter—I, proud father of two sons and three daughters, by whose very existences I mainly ratify my own.

Do I bitch at what Thomas Carlyle called the cash nexus, at how commerce unduly influences public policy, including the environmental decisions that have such an impact on all that I treasure? Yes I do, all the while aware that it was the commercial acumen and effort of certain forebears that now allow me, heir to their significant leavings, to practice the things I practice here, even the bitching part.

But here's an even more damning confession, perhaps: many of the notes for this book—the less vital ones, I hope—were taken on a hand-held tape recorder, an instrument of mediation if there ever was such a thing. What does that make of my yen for things primary, for the purest of physicalities?

I know it's a feeble defense, but by using the recorder I hoped in fact to capture my impressions in the most *un*-mediated way I could. Okay, you'll say: but in that case why not just transcribe the tapes as they were dictated en route? At least then my remarks could hang onto some shred of spontaneity, associativeness, directness. Right?

But I want to write well.

Writing well, or well as I can: that's what I do in life. And even if this is to rationalize again, I'll remind you that any "representation" of primary experience is automatically non-spontaneous, is in fact *anti*-spontaneous. This sad and simple truth applies to the most primitive speech, not to mention to writing—even if you scratch the dust with a stick or design a petroglyph on shale with your pointy flintstone.

Words. Memoirs. Designs. Poems. Cairns. Novels. Totems. Plays. All become, and all at once, translation. So if you're looking, you rambler or you anybody, you Mister Man or you Ms. Woman, for pure "participation in Nature" or in any other instinctual domain, consider yourself a flop from the start.

By this measure, alas, my records of my rambles are torpedoes of the rambles' very values.

In the week before coming here to the Ticino, I saw the full moon come up huge and orange over Mt. Moosilauke. Never such a moon, I thought, and was moved right away to the very translation I speak of. I tried to write a poem next day, one that would do no more than report on the utter moon-ness of that phenomenon. But of course I couldn't. I wanted no metaphor, no appliquéd structure, no beginning and middle and end. If I stopped staring at the roundness and orangeness of that planet, if I began to consider the four rivers of granite that pour down the west side of the mountain, if I note the granite of the summit melting into the low foliage and then into the taller standing trees as the eye moves toward the base, then what had all but knocked me over would be gone, or rather would be turned into something else which I might treasure, if

I did it right, but something utterly unrelated.

So it was better—no, it was crucial—not to write at all.

Which means that I yet carry that moonlight around inside me, and it hurts, like an ulcer. It pushes at the inside of my face; it dares me to talk about it, and Lord, I do keep wishing there were some way to get it into the open, onto the page. Which would be to kill what it was. I know that.

Edward Abbey, author of the matchless *Desert Solitaire*, wordsmith extraordinaire, put all this as well as anyone ever will; to some extent, the inevitability of such failure proved one of his most eloquent themes. Of course Abbey kept right at it. Me too. "We make our meek adjustments," as the poet Hart Crane noted before killing himself (but let's not get to thinking along those lines!). Our contradictions, compromises, self-justifications, strategies, our inexorable flops—of all these are human communications made. Goddamn it all, we were created into this hopelessness, even if what we always wanted was its opposite.

When we choose our subjects, we subject them. They aren't free anymore.

Art 101? Tech 101? Separated (unsuccessfully) at birth. Anyone's birth. The race's birth.

How to be an expert rambler

Sets of rules are nemeses, codes dreamed up by minds that differ from ours. So let's limit ourselves to the one: Ramble.

Ramble for many, many years. Feel the itch and go. As often as you can.

Like anything else, ours is a practice that practice will improve. But it's got to be more than short-lived or half-hearted. Shakespeare, Michael Jordan, Arturo Toscanini, Muhammad Ali, Doc Watson, Max Roach, Willie Mays, Homer, Chagall, Richard Petty, Louis Armstrong, Henri Richard, Rembrandt, Vivaldi, Escoffier, Bob Wills, Martin Luther King, George MacArthur (on whom more in a while)—they all did the things they did, over and over and over, usually on their own, out of anybody else's sight or smell or taste or touch or hearing. Did them for some time.

Then they did them over again, and over and over and over and over. And they got better at those things.

After similar over-and-overness, a rambler in my parts won't earn a reputation like the larger-than-life figures just listed. Not by a damn sight: but he or she will know, when the country is steep (more or less always in my own rambling ground), whether the tree he grasps at for handhold or brake or hoist is healthy and sappy or dozy and treacherous. With luck, which is unlikely to hold all the way, knowledge of things like that will come without too many painful consequences, without his grabbing a sapling trunk that snaps and accompanies him downhill so fast that the instant seems too brief ever to have really existed. I've done that more often than I care to acknowledge. The learner will also be lucky if, like me, he never suffers any really serious bodily woe from that sort of—accident.

I'm afraid we learn caution the hard way. The downhill tumble. Or the cavalier venture onto winter wetland after a snow, for instance, and a subsequent landing, also in a flash, on ice that's been waiting for us just under that slim white mantle. Or the lichen on granite, so benign looking, so beautiful in its subtle yellows and pallors, and the slipperiest thing on earth beside that bog's very ice itself. Hard falls and soft, fierce plummets and slow.

I could go on, but as veterans know, there exist too terribly many other examples for me to chart; no book will help the aspirant anyway. "Always a trap for you in the woods"—that's what George MacArthur told me. He was right.

So only that one rule: Do it a long while.

The rest of becoming expert strikes me as spiritual. The rambling itch just points that way, I find. Which brings me to a point where I should ask forgiveness, with all the sincerity I can dredge up, from those I've already insulted ("Go to hell" indeed!), and from others whom (deliberately or not) I'll go on to insult. Scripture old and new reminds us never to let the sun go down on our anger, and I'm sorry it has peeked into these pages already.

You may say that my apology rings tinny as an eaves-trough, flat as a sports interview, and is shallow as either one. But I do want to beg the pardon, at least, of those congenitally resistant to rambling at all, especially its spiritual dimension. Rather than rebuke them, I ought to offer my compassion—after all, they're missing out on Life.

Life, capital-L? There's that word again, a heavy one like *spirit*.

And who by the Jesus elected *me* (and a few fellow rambler-cabalists) to judge what Life is? I'll try to atone for what may be thunderous arrogance as I go along, and will do so just now by way of yet another digression. I propose it as a parable, and I hope it may cast some redeeming backward light on earlier comments of mine as well.

A day or so ago, I found myself at a grotto. Here in the Ticino, that name refers to a place, usually burrowed into a hillside, where fabulous if basic food is prepared for people who relish... what? Well, who relish a grotto. To speak so makes me sound pretentious, arrogant too, after these few short months in this neighborhood, like one of those awful U.S. expatriates who, on the basis of experience only slightly less meager, refer to Americans as if framing the word in quotation marks, as if in fact referring to odd and slightly repugnant fauna. Be all that as it may, a grotto, though much like an Italian *osteria*, is different. How so? Please, never mind: I'm launched on one digression as it is.

At lunchtime in that grotto, a hang-out for my students too, I was enjoying a plate of pasta when one of the beautiful young persons walked up to my table. Beautiful? Yes, although again her alla moda look—bee-sting lips with cartoony, hard-edged liner (*purple*, for Christ's sake?)—aroused that odd repugnance in me. I wanted to say, all avuncular: "Be as pretty as God made you, fool! Forget the cosmetics!"

Whoa! I thought. You sound like our old radio preacher! I meant the one my country cousins and I used to mock, that hardshell Baptist from Fort Wayne, whole states away, whose radio station had a strong enough signal to reach our center-of-the world campsite.

We were nothing but horny little hooligans, lying out in the fields with our head-swirling cigarettes and our stolen beers under the throbbing planets, longing for Ava Gardner (as if she might stumble upon us in Broad Axe, where we tented, on her way from Beverley Hills to the east coast). But man, you couldn't listen to that goofball minister seriously, a guy who had obviously never in his life experienced this mix of flat beer and pheromones and hopeless pubescent desire (and disappointment). Who on earth would trust *him*, of all people? I remember laughing, howling, puking—such behavior, after all, was "fun"—at his sermons.

At that grotto, I remembered the title of one such sermon: "Don't Bob Your Hair, Girls."

Yes, like kids anywhere, we'd have listened to someone who'd once been as stupid and young as we were then, who'd once been that ready for anything, whose finger- and toe-tips lit up like matches while he waited for Ava, for adulthood, for other things that didn't come then but surely would in his own version of the sweet by-and-by.

For some of us a sweetness did arrive at last. In my own blessed case, something powerful made me up and buy my wife another wedding ring before we flew here, one to go with the ring I gave her in '83, the new band inscribed *auguri per Lugano*.

For some others in that old ragtag circle, life has turned out much differently from how we were sure it would, in our smallness and silliness and booze-bravado. For the beaten, not to mention the dead:

Ave atque vale, Chris, Michael, Harry, Drayton, C. P., Charlie.

We thought everything predictable, and nothing was. We thought ourselves as permanent and prevalent and changeless as those chiseled stars in a black firmament, stars you can't even see now by night, as megalopolis has crept into the hinterland. The sweetness of that air back then, flooding your nose right to the sinuses, the bitterns thumping in the wetlands that are gone forever, even the common crows that roused us mornings, vanished.

But where was I? Oh yes: talking about that pancaked young woman at the Ticinese grotto. She was a stranger, so I hadn't expected her to approach, much less flirt—she didn't—with a man who could be her pa, even—pinch me—her grandpa. It was only friendliness that moved her to speak to a newcomer; but I meant to kick her out of my thoughts and presence as soon as politely possible, if only because she seemed so perfectly to represent the very commodification and consumerist addiction I was complaining about some pages ago.

As we chatted, however, I learned that she was a Serb. Rather, her father was, and married, apparently not all that uncommonly, to a Muslim woman. That woman, wife and mother, died in a military attack from one side or the other, or both, or one of the many, many, too many.

I silently rebuked myself for my earlier knee-jerk assumptions about this girl. As so often, I resolved to guard against such rushes to judgment. I'm bound soon and late to test that resolve again, and when I do the jerk of my knee will no doubt once more be prompted by one of my sentimentalities, which will have a good chance of proving as hollow as the one before.

That pretty young woman. The mating of newts. Woodcock flight. Drive-by shootings. Bluegrass mandolin. Passion for the Meccan pilgrimage. The cut fastball. Monetarism. Free jazz. So much escapes my true understanding, as so much does yours. Pick your own examples.

No one ever owns the central theme. No one's story is unique, or even important—except that it's the story that she or he has lived.

Surrender

I KEEP STUBBORNLY RETURNING, THOUGH, TO ONE OF MY OWN STORY'S BIG themes, which announces itself, if at all, in frustrating fragments: I mean that theme of the spiritual.

The first time I found myself in what natives call The Water Lot, I got the indefinable spirit-feeling. (Freud called it "oceanic," but that doesn't seem right to me in Vermont for a host of reasons.) The Water Lot lies on a small table of land far into the woods; you approach it either by climbing up or down a hazardous, all but vertical face. You finally come on the mini-plateau, where you see old depressions in the hardscrabble soil, signs of failed Yankees' failed efforts to locate a gravity feed of water for the valley settlement below.

Following some more or less recreational urge, making your way there, you'd feel a strange commotion in yourself. Or at least I did and still do, just to think about the valor of those dead prospectors, their dead-serious, dead-end explorations. What would it do to you to see their one "good" hole silted in and mucked over? Its lead pipe has long since oxidized, rusted and broken off a mere few feet from the wet spot; what goes through it isn't a flow but an ooze.

There I stood a moment. Then I lifted my eyes to the scrap of granite above me, the one I needed to climb to move through my rough circle back home. But for more than a moment, for many, I seemed incapable of any movement at all. It was not so much that the climb would be daunting, though it would: rather, the clefts and runnels of the face, bewhiskered here and there with wet fern, which somehow must be clutching such threadbare sod as existed in those fissures, looked to be on the point of coming clear, of spelling something in a language I could read: huge letters with a huge message. A pileated woodpecker for some reason scaled in from a treetop, landed, momentarily clung like a parrot to an outthrust root in the rock. There was a roaring in my ears, as I remember well, not in any way associable with birdsound or wind; not, either, the shallow whine of my chronic tinnitus; something either vast in itself or portentous of vastness of some kind.

And I was ripe for conversion there.

To what? I can't say. Nature's markings in the rock remained what they had been: mere geological bumps and dents. Yet I experienced a physical vibration. Would you have felt that shaking too? Not that I'm better than you if not, only that I'm like you if so.

Rambler, you'd have felt something similar, though tellingly not identical, if you'd followed or led me off-trail above the Beaverhead ten years ago. I was near Bannock, a ghost town that Abe Lincoln once designated the Montana territory's capital, and had climbed from my flyfishing that late afternoon. Uphill from a deserted shacktown, I happened on a series of boarded mine shafts, and I registered nothing less than awe to think of the ardor and pain that went into digging those shafts: humans, antlike against the moraine, boring deep into its iron-hardness with no more than picks and shovels!

Yet you might also understand a curious aspect of all this: because I could see the shaft-entries from hundreds of yards off, for some reason they were less revelatory or iconic than the Water Lot excavations when I first discovered them.

Some would attribute my distinction to the peculiar emotional, geographical and historical bags I lug along, in New England woods or among those Bannock mountains or anywhere, and they'd be more or less right about that. And yet I still assign importance, spiritual or not, to happening on things unforewarned; accident, that "falling toward" I mentioned earlier, sudden surprise—these things are crucial. One does not will himself to grace nor plot a way either. That's not how it works, if it does.

Of course I've said all this already, in so many words.

So many words: yes, I do spend them like a sailor running through his shore-leave cash. And still conclusion keeps running too, always a little bit ahead of me, or a lot. That's why a rambler keeps rambling, despite or because of highfalutin spiritual intentions. Here I mutter things on a page, as if without reflection; but I've actually wound and rewound my tape, considered and reconsidered; not enough—keep going, I say. I find compromises everywhere, as surely as those old dowsers did at the Water Lot, who were in the end betrayed by them; but I go on wandering, groping.

No wonder the diggers at the Lot move me the way they do. Their efforts proved metaphorical without their having any notion that that's what they were. They had other more practical concerns in mind. And yet the idea of the spiritual is like the idea of a backwoods wellspring, isn't it, almost automatically?

Oh, for a pure source, something absolutely original, Emersonian, unrevisable, unrevised.

Where I do my roaming, to be sure, the very notion of originality seems just about ridiculous. This part of the northeast has after all been revised and revised and revised and revised since Europeans came to it, and even well before: the Abenaki burned great tracts of forest to make new forage and cover for the game on which life depended.

At the start of the twentieth century, three quarters of our state was cleared land, the rest woods. The ratio's now inverted.

The farther north you go in any of my three favorite states, the less true. But even in that northness, it's common enough to have been rambling for hours and to come upon the signs of culture, of human care. Even after the rock walls peter out, you will find a cellarhole, often enough in good enough rig that you could use it for whatever brand new dwelling you meant to fit upon it. Even more poignant to me for some reason are other leavings: a sap bucket, say, whose tin is now so thin you might almost spit through it; it is just another snowfall away from becoming no more than idea. The bale still sits in its holes.

On my writing cabin's west outdoor wall, I have hung various other remnants: a length of logchain I found by a teamster's fallen hovel; a couple of metal gizmos that hung in a gutter above a barn door, things with little wheels that rolled in that gutter and allowed the door to slide open and shut; the ring of a snaffle. I'm perverse enough to love the country better now than I would (I guess) were its back hills shorn and populated, but the poignance abides.

And I? The self-styled quester after originality still humps a wildly outdated, heavy canvas tent come down from his father, just because its fabric reeks of things that made him not always and not only happy but at least once made him… mindful. That's still a common term among the old folks; it means a lot of things, one of which is "full of memory." There's a good deal that makes him that way. Including *stuff* after all:

For my whitewater trips (sadly rarer and rarer, aging *bourgeois* that I've become), one of those Kevlar canoes would be much better than the old Allagash- and Dead- and St. John-scarred wood and canvas E.M. White, mine because of an uncle's generosity; the planks in the hull are feathered, not butted, so sand and grit can't get into the seams. "That boat will last forever," as my dead dad said, his brother nodding agreement. Forever? Of course not, but closer to that than I'll come, which oddly pleases me, and far closer than my young father came, which doesn't.

I wear boots till they can't be worn a day longer: what were the ones on my feet the day before we flew to Europe—Coleman, Redwing? Nothing fancy at any rate. I bought them up at Nancy's shop in Wells River when my last pair got rambled out, and I'll do the same when I ramble this pair ragged.

Come upland bird season, I use one shotgun, which I've owned since I was nine and another uncle passed it down. I know, I know: my weapon's a product of the very human ingenuity that in the case of the fisherman with his cellular phone, say, I fumed about. Fox Sterlingworth, pre-World War II, 16-gauge. An old gun, yes, but not old enough for Damascus barrels: technology untwisted that arrangement. The shells I put into the shotgun's chambers are plastic.

I know.

I know that I've never pulled dead-of-winter tits by hand. And I've never set a snare, pulled a bowstring, thrown a spear, cast a net of vines. I know, I know.

Ballistics, Metallurgy. Synthetics. I know, despite my deliberate will not to know, and with a good dose of regret, how obliged my life is to these ingenuities and others, even when I say I want to get as far from them as I can, at least for a time being. Expect me to change that subject when it comes up, to cling to the proverbial bliss of ignorance.

But maybe I'm too rough on myself, because I'm not exactly ignorant—or not only that. It's just that I know some other things too, and know them in another way from a lot of people, especially as we rocket into the 21st century. I'm once more talking about something that slightly resembles religious faith, something equally vulnerable to nonbelievers' jibes: they may well equate it, as they equate religious inclination, with a desire, at once simple and sentimental, not to think. Yet aren't those critics ready to put faith in their very skepticism, about which they themselves can be so grotesquely sentimental? In any case:

How far is a mile uphill? I choose to ask my calves and lungs, not some unearthly satellite.

When does the moon rise this time of year? I ask my eyes and heart, not some gleaming lab instrument scanning globe and sky.

That hum-and-click song of the courting whip-poor-will isn't real to me if I only get it in a book or even on a recording. My spiritual crusade has a whole lot to do, again, with my defense of the *physical* world. I don't know why anyone would find that strange, though I'm sure plenty will.

I should also take time to admit that I was thrown out of every technology course I ever took, which just goes to show how much self-justification really is involved in my reveries, how much fear. But again, I don't really intend arrogance anyhow: if I keep claiming as much, it's because I'm worried I may sound as if I do intend it here and there. Whenever that happens, I try as quickly as I can to correct myself, although I have friends who actually urge *more* assertiveness upon me, urge me to be less wind than rock, to stick up for myself, to take a break from the apologetics.

Okay, I answer, fine—and remain shy of playing the bold adversary. If I say, Go ahead and count your reps of bench press, curl, and butterfly;

go ahead and set the knob on your treadmill; go ahead, keep a computer log to monitor how you're doing; just go ahead and do what you like if it doesn't bother me or mine or our territory: if I say any of that, there's obviously a sneer in my posed open-mindedness, and a private, even sanctimonious pride that I understand the bodily world and the endurance it calls for in a much less mechanical way. But the diffident sneer is the most I can publicly manage, because behind it is a sobering recognition: my boots don't fit all walkers, and probably shouldn't.

Besides, why in hell would I want to convert anyone in the first place? I'm proprietary as a cougar about my rambling territory, more even than I am about any fishing hole or bird cover or deer stand. I want that ground for me alone, have always treasured such exclusiveness, am delighted to have never in all these years run into a single human being on my bushwhacks unless it were a deerstalker in fall or some surprised neighbor whose dooryard or pasture I'd wandered into, off course.

It's getting clearer and clearer that what I'm writing is no field guide or how-to manual. It's a testimony, or again—almost in the theological sense—an apology.

In any case, the way I know what I know, if knowledge is the right term to begin with, seems something about which I'll never be precise. Indeed, I think that's the whole point and style of it. So at last I do surrender any pretense to precision—about anything: it wasn't ever a very passionate goal of mine anyhow. I could tell a long way back that I'd desert it, and you could tell too.

I mean to avoid if I can an all too human tendency: the elevation of his native capacities into virtues and the denigration of his incapacities into defects. For it's surely become obvious that I'm one who makes connections in a peculiar way: it's a good thing, a very good thing and I know it, that not every mind works in that way. The natural world seduces me in large measure because I'm a reservoir of correspondences, flashbacks and flash-forwards, wanderings: a Romantic, it could be, who for all his skepticism and even cynicism about the idea of nature as the mirror of our thoughts can't entirely shed himself of that false dream. One result, as my brother Jake once told me, is that if the phrase "absent-minded professor" hadn't yet entered our language when I was born, some friend would have had to invent it.

With all this in mind, I'll try to renounce my tendency to choose up teams: Us versus Them. That's a sort of bogus precision itself, for one thing, and a habit that's gotten me into hot water more than once. It's a general human habit, maybe, which is one reason the world so often gets in even hotter water.

So now I'm just going to ramble through some territory, reporting actual experiences from two days, a Friday and a Saturday, ones I picked out of my hat. I said a while ago that the will needs to be suspended in a ramble. I'm surrendering it now, to something—to something that I hope is bigger than mere will, whatever the something may be.

I'm going to trust in recollection or the tape recorder or God or pen or keyboard or foolscap—whatever—to take me, and you along with me, to some places worth visiting. Very.

a friday

Swamp

This morning I'll explore a little portion of local wildness I've never studied properly except in winter, when it doesn't show its true nature. I mean the black swamp at the north end of our property, bordering David Placey's 100 acres of remote woodlot.

Why head there? Because the day's itch has swamp in it. I can't yet explain myself better. We shall see.

Even when the ice and snow-cover let me pass over the swamp's real swamp-ness, I often feel some willies there. Not that the place holds anything truly dangerous; I won't fall into quicksand, the idea of which thrilled me to the spine those childhood afternoons with their radio Westerns. Peanut butter sandwich in one hand, root beer in the other, I'd shut my eyes and tip my chair against the Philco's blond cabinet: "Sky King," "The Lemonade Kid," "Red Ryder," and such. I can still feel the throb of the speaker against my upper back.

No quicksand, no, but a similar feeling: my gut clenches a little today, because the swamp, like any swamp bigger than a quarter acre, does have its share of eeriness. Hard traveling too: I picture myself hopping from tussock to tussock, missing as often as I land, sinking to mid-shin and, unsettlingly, even deeper in the mire. Halfway across, the cedars will clump. Even with their needles fallen, killed by standing water, it'll be a job to pound through that stand, which will be thick enough to turn an atmosphere gloomy. I shudder, the cold months in my bones untimely.

As it turns out, despite late summer's plentiful rains, the swamp's all but drained itself. I can't make a bit of sense of that, and the surprise is oddly disappointing: traveling to the far side proves so much quicker than

I expected that I blink like an owl for a moment, adjusting my eyes after a darkness that was never there.

Clear of water for the first time in years, the fallen trunks of the softwoods are actually starting to decompose, as, submerged, they wouldn't do for decades. Indeed, the Abenaki used such trunks to fashion their Connecticut River dugouts. When they headed downstream on salmon and shad forays, they'd sink them in potholes whenever they came to an impassable bar, cross the bar on foot, and raise ones they'd sunk in mud on the far side, reversing the process as they came back north.

From the old river driving days of the loggers, there are still boles of great evergreens at the bottoms of ponds and streams all over New England, ones that were too unwieldy to be dragged over shallows, out to the boom on the main branches of the Connecticut, the Kennebec, the Penobscot, the Machias, the Androscoggin.

I lean over and run my index along the far paltrier trunk of the Vermont cedar at my feet. A chalky, red powder—duff and dust—comes off on the finger. I'm sweating; it's that warm. Still, too: no bird squawks, no breeze in the deciduous canopy on the marsh's borders. A hare, its legs gone white to the elbow with the prospect of a winter that seems far off, drags itself as if arthritically—doesn't bound: no hurry—from one clump of dead, gray cabbage fir to another, north of me 100 feet, unalarmed, slothful.

A rabbit ambling where a blackduck might normally jump vertical, and I'm suddenly and silently quoting from a poem. No, no, don't worry: I'm a poet, right enough, but not the type who prances through wood and dell with couplets dripping off his tongue. It's just that the passage which comes to mind seems to fit this situation so exactly. And even better, the passage is one of the few I have by heart.

You can find it in *The Prelude*, in a section where the young William Wordsworth gets excited, to say the least, by the prospect of crossing the Alps through the Simplon Pass. However, after he asks for directions from a peasant—who, like an Allie Pike, probably thought of the local wonders as pretty much everyday stuff—our traveler discovers that he's *already* made his crossing.

Years later, in his reconstruction of the moment, Wordsworth says that, whether he knew it or not back then:

Imagination—here the Power so called
Through sad incompetence of human speech,
That awful Power rose from the mind's abyss
Like an unfathered vapor that enwraps,
At once, some lonely traveller. I was lost;
Halted without an effort to break through;
But to my conscious soul I now can say—
"I recognize thy glory"....

Now I don't want to overstate myself here. For one thing, Wordsworth was trekking and I'm rambling, to recall one of the few distinctions I've tried to make more or less rigorous. In my very unintentionality, I'm a rambler by choice; Wordsworth is, as it were, forced into the rambler's mode. The distinctions may seem petty; and my point is only that the great man and I seem to share a reverence for imagination: for every person, whatever he or she does, it's a matter of how that faculty gets stirred up.

If Wordsworth failed to find his "high" in nature, he can find it in mind. If my swamp's gone dry today, let me hope my imagination has not. If rambling depends on subverted expectations for its tang, then even a disappointment doesn't have to disappoint the real rambler.

This small zone, whose appearance and odors and terrain and waters I had preconceived, is entirely other than that conception, and once again I find the surrounding hills and even the sky to be framed in a way that shakes me. No, I do not suddenly have the original relation to nature of Emerson's vision, but to my conscious soul I now can say, at least: Well, this is different. This is really different.

I'll not forget it, the mare's tails wispy, but as if stuck against a sky whose blue is so pale as almost to be white as the clouds themselves; this ruddy chalk on my hand, which I smear on my cheekbones like war-paint—I'm a child; and I'm very alone, though not especially lonely.

In any case, having missed the swamp-ness of my swamp, I can still conjure or re-conjure other swampy episodes. Or rather I must. This is one reason why the notion of originality is such a phantom, gone as soon as come upon; because if memory's a great aid to the imaginer, it's even a direr enemy than writing to any man or woman, rambler or not, who dreams of witnessing things *right as they occur*. Not that either enemy lacks its benign aspects, as I'll hope to show as I ramble along.

Just now memory flies me back 50 years. In those days, in summer, I'd follow my Uncle Peter Paine to the Boquette River, which feeds Lake Champlain on the New York side. We went there after frogs for evening feeds by a campfire; I recall watching pale legs twitch galvanically in the pan, then eating those small drumsticks. I remember Uncle Peter's million dollar laugh (he's still the only man on earth whose laughter actually sounds like *yuk yuk*), how it could lighten a gloaming.

I did all the shooting on those trips, with a .22 Remington scarcely longer than my foot is today: at my uncle's instruction, I aimed my scattershot not at the prey but as close to its pad as possible, so that the concussion stunned the poor frog motionless without harming its meat. Uncle Pete and I wore hip boots, although, short and dumpy as I was, he'd usually be the one to play retriever.

I'm sure I'll never go on a hunt like that again nor want to; I wouldn't take any child of mine, either, to do what I so joyfully did on the Boquette. Times have changed, and sensibilities too, my own along with the world's, and there's the scary news that frogs are both depopulating and showing up, as I know at first hand, deformed in our time.

And what lingers is much less the fact of blood anyway than the almost woolen smell of the bog and, more important, the way that smell can resummon the affection I felt for my uncle. I might be able to talk about that feeling more elaborately now, in his hale 92nd year, than then, when it was enough just to be in a certain place with a man who knew that place and what he was doing in it and seemed as fascinated by it and its life as the kid standing next to him with his tiny rifle. Yes, I could talk more articulately about loving that old soulmate now; but explanation, to echo my dear Wordsworth again, doth often seem too deep for tears.

In all honesty, too, another memory of the Boquette also lingers today, even if this morning's ramble hasn't really jibed with it at all. I mean the memory of swamp-dread, which descended on the Adirondack evening as we reached the broad wetland at river's mouth. On the bank cross-stream, hard to see as the darkness lowered, there was the blackened remain of a shack: it had belonged to a woman named Evvie, but it burned before I was five, its owner dying shortly afterward. I remembered nothing about Evvie except that she'd had a frightening face—which now, I'd bet, would look more like a sad one to me.

I somehow intuited that my uncle felt this nameless dread too, and that must have been part of what I felt for him back then, and so must by extension partly account for what I still feel.

Three timbers still stood amid the embers and mulch that was the shack's site. They were of charcoal, ebony, lucent. I'm not sure what about those posts particularly signaled dread, but they did. They were bare as bare could be, no vine to creep up along them; stark they stayed, which was part of what made them awful. As the summer sun dropped directly behind them, their shadows came my way, and it was as though I could see Evvie's countenance—the deep grooves of wrinkle, the dark, carious mouth, the hair as rough as burlap—staring our way. Swamp woman.

I hadn't read any Hemingway in those days, hadn't read much at all besides the Rotogravure comics that bled all over the kitchen table if I spilled my milk there. Yet I'll claim, one's world moving strangely as it does, that I was already looking ahead to "The Big Two-Hearted River," even if I obviously couldn't know that at the time.

Nick Adams, Hemingway's protagonist, having fished all day in the upper reaches of the eponymous stream, decides not to enter the softwood-shadowed swamp he comes to at dusk. He's afraid "the fishing would be tragic in the swamp."

My aborted scouting mission, along with the assorted memories it's kicking up, is related to Nick's situation and presentiment only in the remotest way, of course, in part because there's so little swamp in my own black swamp this morning. Still I know what Nick meant, and I think (who can be sure of such a matter?) I knew something about it a lifetime ago on the Boquette River with Uncle Pete, despite the fact that everyone dear to me was alive and well, even my deaf and blind cocker spaniel Colonel, and as far as I could see God was in his Heaven and all right with the world.

My sense is that any longtime rambler would stand a good chance of catching Hemingway's drift too, because—no matter if real "tragedy" is as absent from his or her life as from mine on the Boquette 50 years ago, no matter even if he or she has ever cast a line—the rambler has found a swamp or two, and so… gets it.

Gets what? What am I after here? Well, I suppose it's that I seem to care a lot less about what are called ideas in man, woman, landscape or book than I care about indelible impressions like the one I've just recollected, and I'm bold enough to suggest that the ramblers I've known share that inclination. They may also find themselves struck like me by the mystical way in which one impression turns out to be a relative of all the others. I'll do as much as I can hope for if I leave you with a few of such vivid impressions, whether I can forge an idea of their interconnectedness or not.

Not that the impressions I wish to leave are exclusively gloomy. You shouldn't suppose I want melancholy to carry the day, or rather the two days, or any day. Above me now, for instance, at the height of Barnet Knoll, the best gun dog I've ever owned, my bitch Belle, has found something. She must have, unless she's run off, as she will now and then do if she's bored. I think, however, she's just uphill, or was a moment ago.

It'll be a downright pleasure to see what Belle's up to, although I know the same thing today that she knows: it's not bird season yet, so she doesn't have to be anywhere near as single-minded as in a few weeks. No bird dog owns as much of that single-mindedness as a pointer: in October, Belle's sense of the target, as prizefighters call it, makes the best heavyweight who ever lived, not to mention the most exalted CEO or scholar or artist, look like he's camping out, as we said when we were kids.

I marvel while I climb, just thinking about all that. Not only in daily daydream, but also in my literal dreams, sometimes I can see as a collective wonder a gang of pointers, going back to my dad's time. They become one, and this one-from-many beast, its musculature astounding, moves in that big, athletic way, head high, tail high. The alders and popple whips take on the white glow of its presence, there's a wind, there's a bird, a shot. Cordite on the air, a smell to thrill me always, whether the bird has flown safe or fallen to the woodsfloor. I am all about pointers, and nothing but, in those reveries. And then I'm all about what I can only call personal history.

The whole way up to where Belle points is make-it-as-you-can, hands, knees, elbows, feet. It's a ledge-and-freestone ridgeside, and I keep telling myself I used to do this sort of thing more easily and vigorously. But my wife always reminds me that I've sung that tune all the decades she's known me; it's why I'm a sap for Wordsworth, who worried about going downhill—at 28!

Wife's opinion or not, at 58 I have to rest now and then on this steepness, but while I do, I keep thinking about Belle: for instance the time, out of season too, in fact plain freeze-to-death, when she stopped and pointed into a tiny blank clearcut. Wouldn't move. Pointed, mind you, over snow just crusting.

She simply stood there, locked up, statuesque as a dog in some rich man's oil painting from a bygone quail-shooting era, if it weren't for the snow cover. I could yank her away, or I could walk past her and learn what turned out to be what: nothing, I dreamed, and, dreaming nothing, I was embarrassed, even if no one but Belle was around to witness: a sure-God something exploded out of that blankness. A grouse. The bird had been hiding under snow, hoping it wouldn't ice up and lock her in, but planning to stay as long as she could with us around. She waited till I almost stepped on her.

In one of Raymond Chandler's Philip Marlowe novels, some punk warns that he could make the detective need some new bridgework. Marlowe replies, "You could also play center field for the Yankees and hit a home run with a breadstick." Belle's point was that improbable, that stunning. To smell a half-pound of partridge from 50 feet under a sheet of white stuff!

Another day, another quotation in the woods. But a *spirit moved across the land*. That's what I'd say about how I felt afterwards, if I thought you'd let me get away with it.

I could recite other jaw-dropping examples as I call to mind all the good dogs I've been lucky enough to be with in woods or by water. But just now, on Barnet Knoll, I discover this particular one digging like a terrier—for a chipmunk. So much for her blue blood. A simple chipmunk. Or maybe, delusional, she imagines that the red squirrel scolding her from the lightning-halved Norway pine behind us is not up there at all: that the squirrel's only a few inches deeper into the ground, just under the crater she's making.

Whatever the case, I'm disproportionately amused, even joyous. Both of us are on a holiday, and not.

I'm really talking about more than random impressions, you see: I want to get at that notion of everything coming together. It's the rambler's version of faith—or one rambler's anyway. Some sense of the shapeliness of things in the aggregate, the good and bad, the predictable and surprising; the phantom red squirrel of Belle's further dreams, or the chipmunk (probably long gone too); the murky vision of murky travel through wetland; my younger children and their mother, all of them at home, busy as I am in their own inscrutable ways, the lives they lead being sui generis, whole chunks of their existences impenetrable by me or by anyone, as chunks of mine are by them or anyone. As indeed the world at large is. But there are times....

It all comes together, must.

Why should this theme of omni-inclusiveness fall on me in certain places, even or especially in inauspicious ones like this? Who knows? No landmark to provoke it here, and that's for certain; nothing but that blasted red pine, hardly different from a hundred others on this ridge; nothing to inspire my grandiosity.

I haven't crossed any Simplon Pass, nor failed to.

Yet there it is again, the very distinction between a ramble and an adventure, "high" or not, whose end is predetermined. I'm inexcusably vain to say so, but the jolt of recognition Wordsworth experienced not far from where I will sit later this year, in Switzerland—the zing of Imagination's "awful power"—seems available to me this morning as a simple low-mountain prospector, as it has on many and many a ramble. The jolt came on Wordsworth by accident; but such accident is what I court.

So far, then, Friday is a fine day.

Is all this stuff "escapist"?

"Escapist? Never!"

Neighborhood genius Robert Frost used those words for a title. He may have been rationalizing. Right now, frankly, that's the only thing I remember from the poem in question. Or he may have been justifying something, just as I suspect I'm doing too.

In any case, I'm ready to thumb my nose at psychologistic label-mongering, and the horse it rode in on. I planned to foreswear name-calling and team-choosing, but I do hope you're not one of those people who actually believe the psyche can be chopped up and served in neat categorical slices. Doesn't every half-thoughtful soul, on pigeonholing a passion as "escapist" or anything else, recognize that he's noticed something relevant—but much more hugely not?

Somewhere one of Bernard Shaw's characters chastises another, roughly as follows: "You want men and women to have their vices and virtues clear and separate. But they exist all of a piece."

John Keats urged the poet, and by extension all persons, to be content with "uncertainties and doubts, without any irritable reaching after fact and reason."

Mighty Coleridge speaks of his own (and his on-again-off-again Romantic pal Wordsworth's) awful power of Imagination as "esemplastic," by which he meant it could take all kinds of contraries into account and yet allow them to fuse.

Even the deeply anti-Romantic Eliot refers to the poet's job as "imagining new wholes," excusing habitually wandering attention like mine as part of "the poet's necessary laziness." The poet, that is, puts together radically diverse experiences, does so as only he can, and the process is one that too much rigor will only impede. (No Eliot fan, I'm still happy enough to have an apology *pro vita mea* from that unexpected quarter.)

Hurray for all those great thinkers! For me as well, I inwardly crow, the sweat on brow and clothing like a magical tonic in this fleet moment.

Who would deny that I'm escaping? Not I. At the same time, I insist that my rambles, even the most obviously fugitive ones, actually end up by proving the impossibility of escape. This perverse truth, I've discovered, results from reflection's and self-inspection's flat refusal just to stay home.

For example: I'm out here this morning partly because my sister-in-law has arrived from the mountain west, along with her children, three years and six months old respectively. I love that family; so do my own children, my wife and even my house dogs: in fact they've all been sufficiently caught up with their visitors that—why not admit it?—I feel a little jealous. No, a lot. In many respects, alas, I'm a bit of a spoiled brat, and I can go far too easily into a pout.

If, then, I start pretending I'm a vessel of virtue, that my marriage and paternity and life in general are nothing but honey-sweet, kick me out the door. But you won't have to; I'm already gone.

I'm not always rambling with my heart wide open to wonder. Sometimes I head for the woods and sidehills because I'm in a funk or even in more genuine pain than that. My mother may be dying. My friend Tony Perry, the best auto-body man in the business, just got word of his lymphoma. Another sister in law is in the gruesome midst of chemotherapy. It's not that there's an answer Out There, but out there is where I'm going. We'll see what happens.

So all right: you can tell me I've escaped.

Will I ever grow up, you may ask? I hope so, I guess, but my hope is only half sincere.

I admit, then, that I needed this morning's ramble for more than literary reasons or exercise, and I'm moot on whether I'm looking for the spirituality I keep clutching after, in part because you don't just go get that. Maybe I just want to go somewhere and mope, and I say as much so as to be honest: if there's a ritual dimension to my bushwhacking, it's not always there *a priori*, and sometimes it doesn't peep out at me at all.

Still and all, I insist that escape's never the whole story, can't be: if it were only that, there are plenty of other walks nearby, ones I often take with my wife, with sons and daughters and more than the one dog and with in-laws and friends and on and on. I've frequently enjoyed what our family calls The Loop, for instance, attended or alone: it's a tramp along twitch roads, a 30-minute circuit from the house and back.

The loggers got done with the Loop years before we even moved onto this property; since then the local wildlife has taken charge of keeping the brush down, especially the whitetails: they don't have the luxury of inventing their challenges, even the minor kind like this one's small ups and downs; no, the deer choose the Loop just to get from here to there and back, from good bedding cover in a nearby fir thicket to a food-rich white oak stand up higher and to the firs again.

You start through the meadow below our house. Right next to the pond, a woods road points due north. Taking it, you go up a small incline, at the top of which on the west side, for several hundred yards, there's a stand of good pine, and the understorey is—save for the odd blackberry tangle here and there—fairly open, so that it looks almost southern, like bobwhite country.

On the east side, the lower shoulder of the Lookout ridge is mostly gravel, almost sand-fine; the turkeys and foxes and deer and the rest leave sign there, but the soil is so shifting that it's hard to read a track, because it collapses into itself almost the moment it's made.

At length, maybe half a mile, you come to a circle of entirely open country, maybe half the size of a football field, where the only growth is waist-high sweet fern. There's a stone ring for campfires there, with a sizeable length of maple trunk hauled near. This is where our 17-year-old and his pals have their tent parties in the warm months. I always smile to see the campsite, not, I'm sure, that it's always good, clean fun that goes on there, or not as the Scout Manual would have it. But at its worst, I surmise, it could be a whole lot worse.

You turn sharp east just past the tent party place, and follow an up and down series of small hills, crowded on either side by thick berrycane; there's a small trickle of water after the first of these hills, and always an interesting footprint of one kind or another in it. The bears like this spot when the blackberries come, and they leave their impressions in the mud and they mat down the canes all around. Sometimes I leave all dogs behind and sneak over the hill, in the hope that I may catch one at his fodder, but—although I've come on a footprint in the mud that was so fresh as to be filling with water even as I arrived, and though I could hear the surprisingly delicate sound of the young bear escaping—I didn't get a look.

At the top of the last rise, you swing back south, against the way you came on the twitch road. It's a game trail you follow, and it takes you within minutes to the Lookout itself, an outcropping that looks down on the oxbow of the Connecticut, so tight and protracted that it must take two miles by boat to go half a mile north or south. On the Vermont side is what's called The Horse Meadow, a vast green expanse that extends from the village up to the Knox's barn, a magnificent Shaker barn, round as a dollar.

Crossriver is the Cow Meadow, about the same size and shape.

The view is beautiful below you. Straight out, it's sublime, with a view to the northeast of Cannon Mountain and the Cannonballs, of Mt. Lincoln off farther, and, straightaway, fabulous Mt. Moosilauke, with its bald dome and its four runnels of granite gulch facing you, full of snow after November, full of rockglint otherwise. Moon and sun love those rifts in the west flank of the mountain; their light is free to perform all the tricks in the repertoire there. If there is any such thing as a sacred mountain, and for me there simply has to be, Mt. Moosilauke is the very one.

I like The Lookout at every hour and in every season, but perhaps best in mudtime and at about noon, when the first true warmth after winter arrives, and the air smells all of sweat and wet and stone and pine—pitch, needle and mulch—and a fellow can unbutton his shirt and soak up the heat radiating off the ledge where he stands. That's what heaven will feel and taste like, or I'll boycott the place.

Of course, there's nothing wrong with what I see and smell here just now on a clear September morning. The mountain's last fringe of brush before the summit is pinking, and the blueberry patches are already the red they'll be down low in another month. Winslow Homer stuff, and all for free.

The family's foot traffic hasn't deepened the game-trail back home, not an inch. This is partly because the path continues to run over lichen-slippery rock much of the way, but also because the deer have been the ones to carve the path, and there are a lot more of them than there are people in our family.

And the deer's behavior is necessarily more regular than ours, because animals cultivate habits to greater extent than even the dullest humans do; it's part of their survival strategy, although a deer hunter, if he figures wildlife habits out, can turn that very strategy against the prey.

Of course, as in that Loop hike, the habitual can also become *us* too, a thing I mean in several ways, one of which is not entirely complimentary to an adult person. I occasionally wonder, that is, if human routine doesn't contain a fair dose of the infantile (or even, aptly, the animal), at least if it turns into compulsion.

One day, while hiking the Loop, I got to thinking along those lines, and the next thing I knew I was thinking of the Graham Cracker, of all things. That cracker was the brainchild of a doctor, a well intentioned one it seems, who believed that alcoholics were driven by their desire to re-experience the breast milk of infancy, to relive the habit of nursing. Such desire, obviously, became deadly when barleycorn stood in for cow juice. So Dr. Graham's famous cookie was meant to replicate the savor and comfort of mother's milk itself.

Laugh if you like, but I won't, and not only because Graham's speculation was kindly motivated: he meant to exchange a suicidal dependency for a healthier one. And scoff if you like at the scientific failure of his experiment too. For my part, I think the doctor was onto something intriguing and valuable.

As a parent of five, I frequently feel suspicious of speculators who are allegedly *more* scientific than Dr. Graham, ones who, I've noticed, are disproportionately childless, Locke, stock, and Piaget. Fact is, infants do not thrive on novelty at all, and I find the notion that they do rather sentimental. If the world were really "always new" to children, as some souls put it so touchingly, then children would probably be unhappy and a lot worse. From what I've seen, small humans' greatest satisfactions lie in repetition. The same story, night after night. The same smell emanating from father or mother. The same look too. (I once shaved my beard after children's bedtime, and the secondborn, five then, cried in horror to see me next morning.)

The word "family" lives inside the "familiar" for good reason: and in the cases of our children, as Dr. Graham intuited, the familiar means the reliable, nourishing breast.

That impulse to familiarity can sometimes move me when I see it in action, in the old-timers around here, for instance, keeping their daily routines as faithfully as an accelerating world allows. The farmers lead the way in this regard, but they are vanishing all over the north-country, are entirely gone 50 miles to the south. Yet they, even in retirement, are regulars, in the truest sense of the term, at the store, the bank, the post office, and their regularity sets the tone for their scions and even for the likes of me and my clan.

Certain remarks above—about my shotgun, my tent, canoe and boots, for example—prove that I've had some such impulse right along in any case. I even wrote a poem years ago in which I figured the knolls out my window as breasts, and not in any erotic way. What was I up to? Maybe the good doctor could tell me. All I know is that some lust for permanence, for abiding sustenance, is part of my way of looking out on the world, even as I treasure the mutability of this region, even as I shudder to imagine, say, a Californian or Arizonan life.

All that said, however, for some reason this morning the habitual just can't do; I must *want* to be reflective, a wish that a familiar trail might fulfill in some measure but still inadequately. I know reflection comes along on any ramble, comes without having to be invited. The familiar leaves one *too* entirely alone with his thoughts; the ramble demands half-consciousness of the need to get back home in some fashion, and it's in this halfway state that one's unexpected meditations can steal into mind, can seep in his soul.

So today, rambling, I'm not escaping. Not at all. What, then? I've left the swamp, gone eastward-upward, found my dog at her play. What next? Always the central question, whose answer is always not there, yet has to be.

❧

There

"THERE IS NO THERE THERE," GERTRUDE STEIN (IS SUPPOSED TO HAVE) said about her native Oakland, California. I borrow her words because by now it's obvious that benign literary theft is, precisely, a habit; also because I want, rightly or wrongly, to apply her non-rambling *mot* to the issue of thereness.

There—always slippery, elusive. Like all definitions, praise be, damn it.

I'm not the only authority on this: much greater woodsmen—the Creston and George and Franklin MacArthurs, the Earl Bonnesses, the David Tobeys—share my assumption about There: that it's protean and finally unfathomable. Those woodsmen keep rambling on, just as I do, but there you are.

No you aren't.

"You can fish a river till noon," I recall Creston saying to me in my youth, "then come back at five and even the Christly water flows different."

Creston had read no Heraklaitos that I know of. He often quoted the old Tory he called Roger Kippalun, but he didn't read much of anything else at all, except price lists for timber or fur. He knew what I know, though, and much, much more.

Creston wouldn't blink to hear that the "swamp" I passed through last winter isn't the swamp, either of fact or fancy, I passed through less than an hour ago. Even Barnet Knoll, where I'm walking now, is different from what it was last week. The hop hornbeams have dropped most of their leaves, holding on to their small florets only, which—food not prime but adequate for wild things—will stick right through the cold months. The florets stand out now: new, minor boldnesses against unleaving limbs.

The one thing that doesn't entirely change here is the fact of wind. It may change in pitch and intensity, but for some reason that I'm too ignorant to divine, however breathless it may be anywhere else, there is always a song of wind in the spot where I stand for this moment.

The song can be stern, especially, I've found, in the last weeks before the snow flies: its rumble is baritone, and you can dream you see the very tree limbs quiver with a kind of fear on hearing it. In April, our windiest month if it isn't March, the wind sings more sweetly, and it bears an odor like old chamois, which I've never been able to identify. Even in listless summer, when the greenhead flies strafe you at every clearing, you can hear a kind of murmur, almost as angry as the flies just made you back half a mile. Why anger in August? "Ask the old Indian," Creston used to say when I posed him unanswerable questions, as if there were one single such shaman out there to explain everything, as there may have been, though I never found him either, or her. Maybe that shaman talks on the eight-month breeze.

I'll head northeast from here along a granite gully that I don't remember, not even if I've hiked it before, as perhaps I have. (I sometimes grimly joke that, once my memory peters out entirely, I'll be able to take an identical walk each day and find it spanking new.) The gully will point me down, down to the Connecticut River plain. Then it'll be a ramble back west, till I hit the Old County Road somewhere above Tink's house.

A pleasant thought, and comic. I chuckle aloud.

Tink Hood, a reader

WE LOVE TINK. NEVER A BETTER NEIGHBOR ANYWHERE, ALTHOUGH—given his crankiness—there are dozens in our town who feel quite differently. He and his first cousin, for instance, live next door to each other; they haven't exchanged a word for years. From what I can get by various means, neither man quite remembers why.

A third neighbor, a newcomer and a flatlander (as people from anyplace besides New England, even if it be Alps or Andes or Rockies or Sierras, are labeled by Vermont natives), got along badly with Tink from the first day, or rather Tink with him. Tink's comment on this friendly and decent guy was simply that "He don't have a gun in his whole house."

That comment shows less allegiance to the NRA—which Tink has probably never thought about for more than a few seconds if at all—or to the cartoon Shoot 'Em Up impulse that Europeans, mostly thanks to Hollywood, associate with this land of ours than it shows a yen for cultural diagnosis. And, whatever you make of it, the diagnosis is on the money: city and suburban folks get understandably nervous around guns, while "we," in one of the least homicidal places in the world, consider them a fact of life. If you don't have a firearm, your chances of grasping traditional Upper New England society are radically diminished.

But I was talking about Tink's temperament, his old-timer's tendency to make up his mind about someone almost on first meeting. The someone gets thumbs-up or -down within a matter of days at most, and it takes a miracle to alter such early, brief evaluation.

I have a half-baked theory about upcountry Yankee behavior, though if it's accurate at all, I think it applies to hardscrabble hill people all over the world. They aren't famed for their hospitality, like denizens of the American delta South, say, where river-borne commerce has always been king, and hospitable behavior therefore a crucial survival skill. Poor hill-folk are understandably suspicious of outsiders, wondering, instinctively, what anyone could be doing in their part of the world, where scratching a living out of bad soil and rough woods is an ongoing and monumental struggle. The famous xenophobia of native Vermonters, Mainers and New Hampsherites may be related to that suspicion.

An outsider must be up to something tricky: why else would he come here of all places? Upper New England, like any other place in our mobile society, now attracts people from all over—the Vermont Senate, for example, now has more non-native than native representatives (which is what's wrong with it, if you ask Tink)—but suspicion abides, even in ghostly guise. My hunting partner Terry Lawson, a mechanic across the Connecticut in Plymouth, has a bumper sticker that reads: WELCOME TO NEW HAMPSHIRE. NOW GO HOME!

Because I've always fished and more importantly hunted, I've been fortunate in tasting very little xenophobic treatment. I've had things in common with the people whose territory I've intruded on; it makes sense to be looking for deer, say, whereas looking for real estate is a different matter. Who wouldn't want to jack a trout out of the upper Connecticut, for further instance? But who'd actually show up with some legitimate business interest in these parts?

Not that I ever waltzed into the Yankee community and got a red carpet greeting. No, that's not how it works. I don't think I've been formally introduced to a hillcountry New Englander more than a half dozen times in my life. Rather, I get to know one or the other by way of one or two of those shared interests: hounds in the case of Allie Pike above, deer in Tink's, turkeys in Doug Merrill's, trout in Ray Hulett's, birds in Joey Olsen's. Then that one will talk to another one about me, he or she to a third, and so on; and in time a group will start to call me by name. Then everyone.

Everybody, of course, will have had all kinds of information about me before anyone calls me Syd. One trades privacy here for a real sense of community. The whole town knows your business; but then again, it knows your children, too, and knows if they're courting trouble of their own or from the outside. Best of all, though it does take time to make friends with people like my neighbors, once they've become your friends you won't find more loyal or helpful ones in the world.

All this, as I say, is changing, for good or ill. Just for example, no one would have thought, 30 years ago, of running for local public office, let alone regional or statewide, before living at least five years in a given town. Nowadays, people no sooner arrive than their names are on this or that ballot. Such public spirit is admirable, I suppose, although it too often seems motivated by a desire to make the hicks come up to speed in one way or another.

As if these towns weren't among the oldest in rural America. As if they hadn't survived since the 17th century without benefit of such salvation. As if their citizens, praise be, whatever their social or economic niches, weren't amongst the least servile or malleable folks on the planet.

A too common aim, in short, seems the transformation of a genuine culture, culture being, after all, more than pictures on a museum wall or higher SAT scores or four star restaurants. Yet some apparently seek to establish a version of modernity and sophistication that can be found all over the nation, to make Newbury, as one friend put it to me, "just like anyplace else."

Having left Fairfield County, Connecticut, Mr. and Mrs. Public Spirit seem determined to reconstruct it in the north-country, and to turn what each has fled to into a replica of what each has fled from.

Forgive me: some of my best friends, as the old saw goes, are newcomers, I don't mean to join the Last One In Club, however long I've been here, and anyhow I meant to be talking about Tink.

My family is literally blessed to have made the cut in our initial encounters with him, and we have relied on him for all manner of things ever since. If I'm out of town on business or pleasure, for example, Tink's aware of it, and he looks in on my wife and children every day to see how they're faring, especially in the harder months, when there's snow or ice or axle-deep mud. If by our children's schooltime he has seen no townward tracks on our driveway, which passes right in front of his house, he hops into his truck to check at our end for flat tires, dead batteries, sickness, power failure, whatever: all the things that can go wrong for a family back in the woods.

And we know it's better to have Tink watching our property than any trained Rotweiler. For one thing, he's insomniac. It doesn't matter what the hour is; no one can just drive through our gate as he pleases: before the intruder (or relative or visitor) has traveled 50 feet onto the property, Tink has grabbed a peek at him and come to his own rather proprietary conclusions. He'll chase a suspect too, because he's not afraid of anyone or anything, as I'll indicate in a moment.

I tease Tink that it's sexual envy that makes him such a watchdog. He wants to know about my comings and goings, not anyone else's, I say, because he's trying to cuckold me, never mind that he's 78 and my wife's 45.

He thrives on such patter. I once telephoned home from the road at 6:30 a.m. Who should answer but Tink himself? He scolded me: "Her and me's just gettin' up."

Tink, native and elder, is an encyclopaedia about our neighborhood's past: he doesn't deal in the sort of information kept by the Historical Society, a fair share of whose members are flatlanders like us, but the oral-historical sort, closer to the ground. A semi-famous murder was committed here in the mid-'50s, for example: a very unpopular local dairyman, bound and gagged, washed ashore downstream on the New Hampshire bank of the Connecticut. The crime was never solved, although a handful of veterans like Tink claim they knew the assassins, some of whom may still be alive, right along.

Oh, he'll talk about all aspects of the case—except the identities of the perpetrators. He'll tell you what a "mis'ble bastard" the victim was, and he'll say he had it coming after all his notorious cruelties to his hired men, and he'll name the villain's name with a sneer. But he won't name anybody else's.

Whether in a vain effort to weasel at him about this affair or just to hear other stories, our children often stop to visit with the Hoods. They know that each of them loves kids, right down to their own great-grandchildren. (In Tink's opinion, "Anyone who don't like kids, there's somethin' wrong with him." He says that a lot.) The children also know that Tink Hood can provide as many hours of entertaining narrative as a listener finds time for.

Tink has also given me useful rambling information: rough directions to old burns, an oddly twinned pair of cellar-holes, whose builders' front doors must have opened right into each other's faces, even several wrecked mills up this or that watershed. Not that he was ever a rambler himself: it's been hard enough for him and Polly to make a living, especially through the Depression, that they haven't spared time for my kind of pursuit. Just make-busy stuff, as they see it, and like Allie, they're a little baffled by it too.

And yet, especially as a deer hunter, a crucial part of being a provider during the lean years, Tink knows the nearby countryside backwards and forwards, up and down. He learned it when it was largely farm territory, too open for my kind of ramble, and later, when thick successor growth reclaimed most of it, former cow meadows clotting up with alder, gray birch, popple, hemlock, cabbage pine, big pine—and so through the cycle.

I know he'll never study written words of mine, unless, like these, they mention his name; never mind—Tink's still, emphatically, a reader. His favorite, in fact his one and only author? Louis Lamour, whose sprawl of work he plows through over and over and over, beginning at the dawn of Lamour's career and pushing on to the sunset until, he admits, he's sufficiently forgotten or blurred the stuff from way back that he can just start over, and no harm.

I now and then ask: "Why not try somebody else?"

To which Tink answers: "Why would I? Once you read him, you don't want to read no one besides."

Fine by me. Fine, at worst, that—as other windows in town and all over the western world go blue with TV after dark—Tink turns on the standing lamp by his recliner (where he catches such sleep as he ever gets).

He's *reading*, by the Jesus!

So Tink's a man of words, unlike the great majority in our time. That's a significant part of his appeal to me, of course, and so is the narrative passion he shares with other aging folks here and elsewhere. That urge to make a story seems to have ebbed in the world of their grandchildren; it's dismissed as a quaintness, if only unconsciously, by the assorted enemies I've dismissed myself, not to mention by the tenure hounds at your local university, who tend to "privilege" (one of their cant words) an ancillary inventiveness over the real variety, and who—safe in their alabaster chambers—have the nerve to call narrative a "reactionary" political gesture. (Thank God we have *them* to deliver the oppressed and the poor!)

But I was saying, this old boy just relishes a tale, in the reading and in the spinning; he thrives on the worded life, so to speak, which means among other things that he lives in, by and for anecdote. He tells it and makes it both.

He's damned good at both too.

When our family moved to town, we heard—from him—of a feud he'd had with still another neighbor (another nice guy too, as it happens). The fellow's spaniel kept roaming; he'd more than once dug holes in the Hoods' vegetable garden, the jewel of their existences, and as productive a plot as you'll see in any horticultural journal.

Tink warned the dog's owner to keep him "to home, where he belongs," and threatened to do some shooting if there came another raid.

Bad blood in the air, and of course the end of conversation between Tink and one more local household.

At that time, I happened to be training my Belle, who was just at the right age. I'd bought a mess of penned quail, and would plant them one by one for her to hunt up and point; on the flush, I'd shoot off a blank pistol, so she'd associate her job with gunfire. Easy stuff and in her case only half necessary: a true gun dog more or less trains herself. Breeding; genes; miracle.

This was in September too. One morning, driving my second son to school, I noticed I'd left the gun and a full box of blanks on my front seat. If we slowed down by his house, Tink was bound to walk—or more accurately trot—over for a chat. So Jordan and I hatched a plan.

Here's what we knew: that Tink, repeat, was always good for a "visit," a word whose full implications seem inexplicable to most flatlanders; that in their retirement he and his wife Polly haunted the local flea markets, where they bought old furniture to restore and resell; that at one of these markets Tink, for whatever oddball reasons, had picked up a life-sized, plastic St. Bernard, which he'd stuck on his lawn in an orange collar with a tag reading SYD; and most important, that we had that pistol handy.

"How you like my new dog?" he'd been shouting for days as I drove by. I'd give him a thumbs-up, or another finger sign just for play, then I'd keep on trucking. I felt guilty right along, but it was a busy period for me right then, and I always seemed in too much of a hurry to jaw with him about his damned dog effigy: if you stop at roadside, or anywhere, for a visit with Tink, you have to expect to put in some time; anything else is a greater rudeness than a mere wave.

Jordan loaded the blank pistol. When Tink came down for his hobnob, he'd lean into the cab as always, resting his elbow on the passenger side windowsill; we could count on that. Jordan would tell the old buck how his pet had been roaming, how we'd had enough of it, by the Jesus. Then he'd stick the barrel just under Tink's nose and fire all six rounds.

Jordan is a masterful mimic, and was even then, at eight years old. He spoke the upcountry brogue as well as Tink himself did. "That dog's been messin' round our garden," he said in mock anger.

"Has not!" Tink replied, faking indignation.

"Has too," the boy continued, "and we're fed up on it." He blasted away, as planned, right by Tink's face.

Tink didn't twitch or blink. He just looked over at his St. Bernard for a moment, then he turned back: "Missed 'im."

My son laid the gun back on the seat, its barrel hot as a hinge. As we went on to school, he said through his tears of mirth, "That's the toughest old man I've ever seen."

"Maybe the toughest guy, period," I told him through mine.

In short, Tink is more than literate; he's a born entertainer, a historian… and as I've said, pretty puzzled by this thing I call rambling.

"Why'n't you work a little?" he'll chide me, only half-jokingly, my notion of work being a lot different from the real thing in his view. "Then you wouldn't be *looking* for your exercise!"

If I could get him to read the rest of these pages, maybe he'd know I do some work after all. Maybe he'd understand what the work's for, and why the rambling is part of it. But he won't do any of that—and no, he might not understand if he did.

But Lord, how could I make a judgment on which of us has a saner take on things that matter, on whose "education" is superior?

On education

I once told my favorite grad school professor that I'd been thinking about a life in the outdoors. Not part time, either—full.

"Why would you want that?" he wondered.

The man was my intellectual hero—no competition in that respect, not even at mighty Yale. But I imagined that his notion of wildness was maybe based on something like the pigeon droppings that coated Goethe's statue in Central Park; but then again, he'd written the best book on my roving/rambling poet William Wordsworth that had ever been written, or ever will.

Go figure, as they say around Central Park.

"Why would you want that?" he repeated as I stood there silent.

I didn't really know, I mumbled. (I was already proving how hard it is to define the "itch" I've talked about.) Then I muttered something else about wanting to be a cartographer. I never let on what I really wanted to be, which was the sort of cartographer's *assistant* I'd met twice in my young life.

The first was a woman who rode her horse up one sublime Colorado game-track after another, into territory still not perfectly charted by USGS, taking notes: her bedroom ceiling in the better months showed nothing but stars.

The other cruised the woods of northwest Maine to similar purpose; or rather canoed the waters—he was helping to update maps too, these ones of islands in the Allagash chain.

I still envy those two a little, even if their regions are now too damn thoroughly charted, too damn thoroughly chopped, including the islands. (It didn't occur to me for some reason that the work I dreamed of back then was actually *anti*-wildness work.)

No, I mentioned neither of these people. If I had, Professor H.'s question would have been even more vehement: Why on earth choose a life like that? To this day he's a man whose brilliance humbles me, and whose decency to me feels horribly unreciprocated these decades later. Still, though, he wouldn't understand even the compromised version of outdoorsiness I've managed to enjoy.

"If you are patient," he cautioned then, "you'll have a choice of academic appointments. You'll live the life of the mind. That's what you're for, after all."

The language sounded funny. It seemed off. And not only because—like so many families of valued thinkers in modern America—his had been among those hounded all over the map by the Nazis, meaning that he wasn't a native speaker of English. No, it was the *content* of his remark that rang odd.

"The life of the mind"? Bullshit, I thought, both right and wrong.

I was right that the guy wouldn't have any idea what I was talking about if I remembered that Colorado woman and that Mainer out loud; and I was right that—no fault of his, God knows—he'd never exactly exercised "choice" himself as a young man. But I was surely and spectacularly wrong as well. I didn't see good advice even when he slapped me with it.

No, that's wrong too. His advice was only half-good, as it's turned out. The professor—no fault of his either—misjudged a lot of my mental makeup, but he also read things in it that I myself had missed. He may even have sensed, and never mind the would-be woodsman in me, how stupid I'd be to repress an apparently inborn domesticity, which I couldn't in any way imagine at 22. He definitely sensed that—wherever I might roam, land or sea or foam—I'd need artfully arranged words, my own or other people's, almost as much as I'd need food and drink.

Years later, I cringe a little over how blind I was in these respects. But I hold to one claim I made back then, clumsily as I must have done so: that The Life of the Mind had to be more than a scholarly life. For me anyway.

Please don't take what I'm about to say for one of those anti-egghead, Huck Finn "Lite" anecdotes that always seem to get a chuckle from Americans. (They were a staple of Ronald Reagan's repertoire, for example). I'm grateful for every hour of schooling in my own repertoire. But in any case, Uncle George MacArthur—not my real Uncle, though I and my siblings called him that—once warned that, although he envied my sort of education, he feared it would block me from getting other kinds.

George was also right and wrong, and he had his reasons for what I'd call the wrong part. Because his parents needed one more piddling woodsy income a long lifetime ago, he'd quit school half that lifetime before I did. He left after fourth grade, and I after umpteenth. And yet he was, I'll tell you what, one forevermore learned old boy.

Get out there, he was saying. And that counsel was right. At least—though less vividly than George: lumberman, poet, tie-maker, trapper, songwriter—in one way or another I've tried to follow it, to get out there. (Old slippery There again.) I've done other things too, clearly enough: my extended stays in Europe, say, are not common to professional Paul Bunyan types.

All that notwithstanding, as I've shown and hope I'll keep showing, for me the Life of the Mind has been a rambling sort of affair. Just now for instance the mind meant to take a breather up on Barnet Knoll; that's where it was headed, all right, along with the body—and here I've fetched up in grad school and in Colorado and Maine and with Uncle George and in some self-dispute as close to philosophy as I'll ever come. If I linger longer, I'm apt to quote or even write a poem.

Here I am, wherever, lost in a half-hopeless search for the thereness of There.

Maybe it does live back with Uncle George. Or with Uncle Peter. Or with Creston MacArthur, for whom my older son is named. Or with this good dog or that. Or with all of the above and more. In any case, I know that looking for Thereness is looking for Hereness too, just as looking for Now means digging up Then.

So, among other things, I'm here, as always, off to see the Isness, the wonderful Isness (the Itch-ness?) of Was.

***

There (reprise ii)

Later along, it will have been raining so hard one afternoon in the Ticino that, rather than make the 25-minute climb home to Hesse's Montagnola, past the somber cypresses flanking the graveyard of Sant' Abbondio (where Hermann lies in his splendid, ample, lonesome corner), rather than expose myself to a sopping, I'll call a cab.

If the Swiss have a supreme reputation, it's for punctuality. Of course, these are Italian Swiss (*which is to say, quoting Uncle George's*

saw, they got altogether different guns). Whether for that reason or not, my driver's sense of time will prove, like my Italo-American wife's, rather—Latinate.

Now I'm not normally greatly troubled by such blitheness, but on that day my wife will have left the house, tending to other kids' needs, and our 12-year-old daughter will soon arrive home from school. And, if this guy doesn't show up soon, there'll be no one to greet her there.

So? (As my students, Here and There, might ask.) Big Deal.

For me it will suddenly be every bit of a Big Deal. Immense in fact. I don't like the thought of Catherine's (or her brothers' or sisters') feeling anxious, even though I'm sure my own fretfulness, and worse, my fitful need to control the planet, can make them as anxious as anything else.

But Catherine's frame of mind won't really cause my worry, because she's an unusually calm and collected child, indeed—for all her youth—scarcely a child at all in her dealings with the world; and, although you no more need to lock a house in smalltown Ticino than in smalltown Vermont, she'll know where the key is, will have a place out of this rain.

So I'll try to make myself honest about my own distress, recognizing that its motivation isn't really thunder, lightning, or downpour at all. Suddenly I'll understand that, for some dim reason, I'm aching just to love her, to squeeze her with my burly but aging arms. In fact I want everyone home: my wife the attorney, my oldest boy the writer, my oldest daughter the social worker, my 16-year-old son the student-athlete, Catherine herself, the artist, and the female Sydney, nine-year-old family character.

I'll suddenly want the familiar as often as I claim to want its opposite; I always have, for all my wildness-thirst. I'll see my good fortune in owning a life well blessed in both, at least as gratifying in the coming back as in the going out. I'll vow to remind myself of this when I need to—which is much more often than it should be. I've been neither intellectual nor woodsman entirely, but I've been enough of both for each to inform the other, to help me savor what I savor. And I've gotten all kinds of other things into the bargain.

So where is the cabbie, and where just now is Catherine? I'll ask the double question over and over, having perhaps been infected by my host nation's Angst.

Angst? Not a word one tends to associate with Switzerland, I know. But a German colleague will ask me how else I'd explain, say, that Swiss law requires any new construction, public or private, to include a bomb shelter? And in the bowels of San Gottardo, just north of where I'll be staying, the Army's in turn obliged to keep 24 months' worth of food for the entire population of the nation!

As my colleague will joke, "Neutral little Switzerland... prepared for World War Five."

All this may be connected as well to Swiss xenophobia, which is rather well known, and in fact makes our Yankee's look pretty tame. Switzerland has the most restrictive immigration laws in Europe. (It will take me, a declared temporary resident with contract in hand, with no criminal past, with full credentials, three months to get a permit to work six.) Many Ticinesi, for all the great kindness they'll show my family, are even contemptuous of their brothers and sisters in language, the Italians.

But then, as a friend from Milan always insists, "The Swiss don't like anybody." My German colleague's wife is Ticinese, and according to her, he'll report, the Third World begins at Ponte Tresa, the Italian border town three miles away.

An extremely rare instance of violence will be much in the news during our stay, and will arguably be xenophobic in nature too: the Lugano police, in plain clothes, in unmarked cars, no strobe lights active, will shoot a Serb on the city streets, and will, it appears, have a good deal less to answer for than Stateside cops would certainly have. To be sure, the victim had stolen a car, may even have been part of an organized ring of thieves. He was, nonetheless, unarmed.

Where was I, I'll ask myself as so often, and how did I get here? I was only worrying over a daughter in a storm. What am I trying to connect to what? More than I'll be able to tell, even if I won't even remember, for instance, whether Catherine has ever actually been with me on Barnet

Knoll, recently or in bygone days when I backpacked her through the woods, like all the other children before and after, winter and summer. Was she the one I toted that afternoon on Stonehouse Mountain when the sugar snow of late February came down all around us, surprisingly powdery, and the daytime owl blinked from a branch, and I thought how wonderful and somehow right the world was just then and maybe forever? And how do I ever forget those moments of accurate vision, those "God-shots," as one friend calls them?

Today, how all connects to all doesn't matter, really: odd faith simply insists that one day, wherever I happen to be, I'll look back and see Barnet and Catherine and all the other children together, and linked to here and there and everywhere as well: to woodsy Thens and to the Today that will come to south Switzerland as I mope in the rain and to the death of a Balkan felon and to a time that precedes and includes all my sons' and daughters' births—and to everything and everyone else I've cared about in my life: to my wife and to ecology-so-called and to poetry-so-called (mine or others') and to rambling-so-called (mine or others').

Everything comes together, I say say say again again again. I'm right too, because why else would such a wide range of stuff, past, present and future, collapse into the sort of ache I'm suddenly feeling on this Yankee hill? It's like the beautiful pain I've had on watching a baby as he or she popped out of the womb. Every time, I've made a *whuff!* from my chest cavity. *Whuff!*—for the slightness of my part in such miracle and exertion (they don't call it "labor" for nothing). *Whuff!*—for the whole wide rambling world's fragile connections, fragile flesh.

Where is this damned cabbie anyway? I'll say say say again again again.

Well, here he'll be, all apology, the traffic awful at this hour (as any older hand in the neighborhood could have predicted). Here he'll be, a man so decent and courtly that, against local custom, I'll leave him a fat tip.

And, because my daughter won't yet be home when I get there anyhow, some schoolchums' amusement delaying her, I'll sit myself down

at the dining room table, crank up my wretched recorder, get back to where I said I'd be moments ago.

"Wow," I say, as if I didn't know better.

Wow?

Whuff?

The first responses to intense experience always seem crude, hardly verbal at all—which may or may not tell a writer something.

And yet I'm wowed, all right, because the game trail I've struck is, well, striking. It's completely new to me, though obviously a long way from that to the game itself: tracks have turned even this fairly dry stretch of earth into something like a stockyard's.

If I were still a deer hunter, I'd set up right here, behind that punky yellow birch blowdown, on an accommodating boulder-seat, soft with moss and with rectangles, yellower than the birch itself: a pileated woodpecker's calling cards. A good spot for hiding.

And hide I do, for no reason on earth, except that I want as usual to see what arrives, from outside or inside.

All these signs of hoofy traffic assure me that a decent buck will eventually come along if I wait, even out of season. He'll have to. Every buckhunter knows as a matter of course that this kind of certainty doesn't mean a hell of a lot; I might sit here from now right through the rut and not get the shot that I plain knew I'd be getting.

That's one advantage a rambler has, even if she or he has never hunted one hour: thinking about a buck, or whatever else, can be a kind of seeing, the kind that comes to me now: in mind, I can change everything to later autumn, and then can look 20 yards uptrail. Love-hungry, the big fellow stands on two legs to rub a brow-gland against that low beech branch; he goes jigging on a little way, arches his back, drops a jot of deep orange on the snow.

He grunts, he farts, he cuffs the turf, he capers like a goat, he whirls.

Now that deer doesn't know I'm watching this display. He doesn't know that anything observes him, let alone a human. Still, he makes this big damned show of himself, as any male of any species, for better or worse, tends to do. He's practising. He's posturing, as I think we may charitably call it.

From nowhere, I suddenly recall a privilege—a blessing, really—that came to me years ago, when I watched something much rarer than a whitetail in rut: the courting ritual of two whippoorwills. The birds' song in the clearings was so common back then that we hardly paid attention to it, and could actually get annoyed by it sometimes when we tried to sleep. A dear friend of mine, a true flatlander, once bought one of those obscene blowup dolls and hung it out his window as the anti-whippoorwill equivalent of a scarecrow. (The unthinkable and hilarious part of all this was that it worked!)

Things have changed, sorry to say; no need to shoo that singer off now. But even in those days, the birds' courtship was just what it was called in the several ornithology volumes I consulted that evening: "obscure." The expert I phoned at a local center for wildlife study used the same term.

The hen picked gravel, busier than a one-armed paper hanger, as my grandmother used to joke. The cock made a hum-and-click sound, almost electronic, as he puffed himself big and gaudy and strutted around. I remember being thrilled among other things to discover where that noise came from, because, more than any song, it had so often kept me awake and puzzled in early summer. Now I had it forever, and I'd see a whippoorwill whenever it sounded, would see it even as I lay drowsy, just on the point of sleep. So the bird would keep on waking me up, but who'd complain?

Now and then, the female glanced up, like a languid, veteran dog at some passerby, no more impressed than that—which made the cock crank his dance up a notch, or several, till he looked ready to tumble out of his party plumage. The hen would notice his hoopla or wouldn't, depending, I suppose, on some "obscure" avian mood. Then back she'd go to her pecking, business as usual. The time dragged enough that I almost feared for the antic cockbird's health.

Was there some glorious coupling later on, in the wee hours? I hope so, but I never saw it. In any case, though, before sleep fell on me as I lay against a stump, these preliminaries brought another revelation: I was watching a caricature of *human* sexuality! At least the adolescent variety, if personal memory serves.

I was watching "Men."

I was watching a "Man" as he counted on radical extroversion to carry the day; I could think of parallels from high school:

—"Billy Bullett's car? It's a dog. Want to ride in one that does zero to 60 in eight flat?"

—"James Dean? You kiddin' me? Want to feel some real triceps? I been lifting."

—"Him? He's a farmer! How about this new Hawaiian shirt I bought, these sideburns, this Bulova, these boots, this belt, this bike?"

And "Women," meanwhile? Every Woman is thinking about more important things, at least to her. All of which means that Men are a sorry set of sadsacks—not that the sadness of such sacks is any the less sad just because it's so stupid.

The stupid are always with us, a sorry fact in its own right, and, though perhaps mostly, not only a male issue. To be against stupidity in yourself or other people is like being against winter or nightfall: it'll be there, even if you hate it.

I felt something when at last I woke up, stiff and sore in shoulder and neck, and at length recognized the glow at the foot of the old pasture as my house. I felt something as I lay in bed a few minutes later. But it wasn't a feeling of stupidity.

Perching here on my comfortable stone, do I feel stupid now? Not really. I've been sitting, yes, but hardly idling, much less escaping; I've been straying right along, leaving one trail, getting onto several others, coming back, slipping away, returning. And I insist that each of those trails is a branch or tributary of the next, that you slander me therefore if you accuse me of non sequitur, let alone dullness. Everything here follows everything else. And it all makes a kind of sense.

You might try to drag me back to that first path, the one I discovered a few steps and reflections ago, my phantom buck having passed into whatever spiritual corner I've dreamed up for him. All right, I say, I'll go—knowing that simple sort of resolve never quite works. I get up from the boulder, once more a bit stiffly (how long have I been here, for the love of God?), and before I can stop myself I'm at another detour: round and round I go. Again.

I did think of a buck deer, probably because hunting and rambling are kith and kin in my experience; they inform each other. I know, however, that they don't do that for every rambler. And here's a harder thing to acknowledge: maybe they haven't even done it for me. That ought to be a shock, but all I've managed, really, is to re-arrive, maybe a little more forcefully than usual, at an old recognition: the itch of the trigger finger and the rambler's itch may be related, but they're not identical. Aim is poison to a ramble, as I insisted right off; the hunter aims in all senses of the verb.

No, much as I've loved the hunt (and still do, even if the image of a real buck doesn't fire up the man as it did the boy), it's not like rambling for *anybody*. "Success" is a much different matter in each pursuit.

Pursuit? Well, Latins call hunting The Chase (*la caccia*, *la chasse*, *la caza*). That's a notion central to both callings, but....

But why bother to get any more lost than I am, this time in etymologies? No, I'll chase onward. It's *hot* pursuit, or it feels that way, even if as usual I'm not sure what prey I'm after.

I brush the pecker-chips from my backside, hike a bit, and almost before I'm aware of it, I'm headed harder, much harder, downhill toward the river, which means I do have a bead on where I'll be headed for the next hour at least: unless something turns me, as it might, I'll strike the abandoned train rails at valley level, follow them north towards Wells River, then climb this same palisade, completing a rough circuit.

After I'm on top again, maybe I'll figure out just where I've been and where I stand. I'll discover it there. Up there. Somewhere up at the top.

Above the tracks

I HAVE TO CONCENTRATE TO GET DOWN THIS FLANK UNSCATHED, AND I mean to. Of course my old man/Wordsworth consciousness sneaks in beside me as usual, and I must guard against its distractions—which, however, I halfway welcome. It simply wants to tag along to the tracks, I guess, which I won't reach without crossing the beaver flowage just ahead.

But heads up, eyes peeled, and so on.

The beavers' source of moisture is the failed Water Lot, of all places, some 40 yards off and up to my south. That's a little heartbreaking as I think about it for a Wordsworthian moment. How modest the old folks' flaws in speculation really were! They must have stood where I do now, a baseball throw away from their abandoned diggings. How could they not have stood so? A mystery, I say, who of course wasn't involved in their dowsing. In any case, I see, the history of a township could have turned out differently, if they'd only made a better or just a luckier gamble.

Would that have been a good or bad difference for me, avid rambler? One thing's certain: if the old-timers had placed a winning bet, their good fortune would sure as hell have changed mine in the bargain, not that they could dream me up then as I dream them up now. My wanderings today, with all the emotional responses that accompany them; my past rambles and the ones, I hope, to come—all these would have been changed, one way or another.

I'd have found other trails and feelings, of course. It's just that I can't quite imagine them, because I've never seen their landmarks, never thought the thoughts they'd bring on. My life would be another book than it is, and that idea turns me unaccountably sad for a moment.

But would I have been different? I can't confidently say, any more than I can evaluate what I'd have become if I'd taken the job offered to me in Washington State when I was starting out rather than one in New England. Different wife, perish the thought; different kids and friends and neighbors, ditto. Curious, but sad too.

Of course, in a different state, with a different family, on different trails, I'd still be the one who never did any equivalent of pulling Yankee cowtits before dawn in January, never experienced anything like the *whock* of Bessie's hoof in my breadbasket. Or if I did, it was in my gentleman-farmer uncle's dairy shed when I was a boy, and that was only a diversion, on which the grim hand of necessity imposed no burden at all.

I'd remain the same old me, one who more or less freely chose a "burden," a term that seems both laughable and pretentious: it's to feel vague empathy for all sorts of things and beings, and then to record what I feel in writing, and to imagine that I do that above all for The Right People.

But who, exactly, are they, these right ones? Oh, please don't ask.

Please let me ramble. Please don't overload me with *ethical* burdens too. I've made more than one painful confession already. Leave me alone.

I'm at the most treacherous part of a hill just now. Leave me to deal with it, and with my claim—equivocal, impassioned, lazy, heartfelt—that it all comes together somewhere. Here or there. Maybe here and there both. And now and then are in the mix. And tomorrow too.

If I can scramble down this shaley slide right ahead of me I'll be on level ground. Again I tell myself to concentrate, but—never mind my comments just above—old hunts won't leave me alone. Once I *flung* myself down a slide like this....

A boy, dogless, I'd shot a grouse, which fell into a years-dead quarry, relic of better times for the local stoneworkers. I stood in my tracks for a moment, amazed that another kind of quarry should die, too, all because of something that a single puny soul like me could do. Then I just skated down that bank!

There was water in the hole, turned green by limestone. Even in death, a bird kicked up a sad little foam on the surface; curled autumn leaves, which I didn't yet banally associate with time's velocity or with fragility, sailed around in the gusts. I waded hip-deep to retrieve my trophy, not knowing till I clambered back up that I'd torn a trouserleg and a knee on one of the ruined pit's shards; my pants showed a scarlet stain, bright as any of the maples overhead. But I didn't waste time inspecting the wound: it was bound to be trivial, I figured, rightly; I could forget it, I figured, wrongly.

I said something about the Isness of Was, but there's obviously the Wasness of Is too.

I mention all this not because I intend a lot of guff about my "innocence" (or its loss), but to illustrate all over again that the rambler will have his or her associations. You might as well try to stop the tsunami, the earthquake, the cyclone.

Of course, rather than skating now, I pick my way down, not without recognizing how I've become—so quickly, it seems!—the sort of cautious old guy I made private fun of as a kid. But hell, I have a wife now! Sons! Daughters! The full miraculous rest. Back then all I had was my immortality. I've made a good trade, I think: all that delusion for what I have now—and nothing wasted. Nothing.

But look how I creep along here!

Human waste

THAT WHOLE WAY DOWNHILL JUST NOW, I FELT A NEED—FORGIVE THE crudeness—to move my bowels.

My bird-hunting pal Joey Olsen once dubbed me Professor Woodcock: "You're just like him," he said. "Can't land in the woods but you have to leave a little splatter."

He was right at the time, a decade and some ago. Mine was a psychosomatic response, I'm convinced, to a profound desire on my part not to leave that splatter. I've always been, to put it in mild terms, unhappy about a crap in the woods; at one time, the idea caused me actual dread, some premonition of personal doom. So of course I couldn't avoid thinking about crapping whenever I broke into a cover: I'm reminded of Tolstoi's claim that no one he commanded to "sit in a corner and not think of a White Bear" could successfully follow the order.

I'm more or less over that nuisance neurosis by now; yet, for Joe (and a few others, both to my amusement and embarrassment), Professor Woodcock has stuck with me right up to the moment I write this—write it for Joe and a few others, too many of them too many miles away.

Doom? Maybe I exaggerate, at least this time, because what follows on the tracks turns out to be so much literal crap.

Strange, though: I believed I was all over it, but the threatened feeling comes to me again, here on a random Friday in Vermont. Something's on my mind: what? Well, I haven't been thinking so, but I guess anyone my age must wonder, at least subconsciously, whether a third day will be available, or a fourth, fifth, 50th, 100th, so on.

I can almost see Joey smile at my train of thought, at the way a physical need to excrete has gotten me, as it were, into emotional deep shit. But I can go on inventing these lame puns as long as I like; the fact remains that what I'm discussing doesn't feel like a joke—or not entirely. I've never been able to talk about it, really, never been able to tell my very best friends how insignificant I've seemed to myself over the years whenever I eased my insides in the outdoors. Maybe it's the awkwardness of the position, my defenselessness in it, that brings on the spiritual chill: I could ramble all over the inner and outer worlds, but like everybody else I'd still be so damned much smaller even than the diminishing wildness of the small earthly world I pass through.

I think to myself: anyone who saw me in this, my most humbling posture might be seeing me at my most real.

The downward slide left no opportunity for relief of *any* kind. Or have I been waiting to reach the railroad bed for other reasons? These tracks have lain unused for several years now, but maybe I've imagined an excuse for my own pollution in a place where a more general human pollution has at least existed before. Don't get me wrong: I like a train, and I miss the one that traveled here; but for the natural world that train is basically a gout of poison fumes, noise, vibration, erosion, herbicide and the awful rest.

Wherever the truth may lie, my mind working haywire as ever, at the tracks I—contain myself. I walk the bed for a few hundred yards, and then another few. Yes, I'm in a human zone, even if it's become dispossessed; now that I'm here, however, I find myself looking for a non-human one. There's the old proverb about greener grass; this may be an odd place to assess its wisdom, though probably not.

In any case, my metabolism is giving me one set of orders and my immortal soul (la dee dah) another. What I seek is—well, "symbols" strikes me as a term too cheapened by over-use, and too grandiose anyway for the mere filth I plan to deposit somewhere nearby.

In my madness or whimsy or whatever, though, I guess in fact I *am* looking for some emblem of spiritual permission here. Too wild for that above, too traveled here below: ludicrous dilemma! Do I really imagine some sign or wonder will validate a rambler's crap?

Absurd.

Presumptuous.

Yes.

More and more gut-crampy, I walk on till at my feet, among the frost-heaved rails, dislodged spikes, splintered ties, clinkers and cinders, I see the femur of a young deer. The bone isn't "bleached," as more conventional narrative would require it to be; it has an iodine-ish shade, and retains tufts of hair on ribbons of parchmenty hide. The bone speaks of fairly recent life; it hasn't become an abstraction yet. The hooves glint; they're shoe-polish black and delicate. Nothing here to suit my purposes.

Off left of me, west, a standing pool, and a standing heron: impaler of trash fish, frogs, salamanders. The bird's comely enough, to be sure, but too common for literary ambition, even too common to deserve attention. Otherwise, he'd seem exactly appropriate: he's a real manure-spreader, that one; in fact they call him a "shit-poke" in these parts, a corruption of "shy-poke," his less ignoble nickname. But no, I think in my bizarre snobbism, he's not adequately totemic. I'm indifferent at best to the so-called Great Blue (who's in fact the size of a frying chicken under all that plumage, and slate gray to boot).

In the '50s and '60s, I suddenly think, I showed the same indifference to an osprey. We're told that the fish hawk, as the bird's also dubbed, is mounting a rally, but you could fool me about that along this stretch of the Connecticut. Some time back, DDT and other pesticides made the ospreys' eggshells so fragile that the chicks broke through too early to survive; and damn few of these fabulous raptors have made their way back to where we live.

Eagles, meanwhile, are making a genuine return, even in thickly settled portions of the state. Fact is, I'd be more excited this morning by a fish hawk than by our bully-boy national bird. Rambling further west two weeks ago, I had a chance to test such a claim: first an eagle scared a mess of Goldeneye off Harriman Pond, stooping but missing; then it flew north, out of the country, over Blue Mountain. Afterwards, if not by much, an osprey—probably relieved to know that its bigger cousin was gone and wouldn't steal its catch—dove to the water. Stupefying, as always.

I stood and watched, my breath short from my uphill hike, and something else too: I followed the osprey out of sight. Having streamlined its catch—mud-chub, dace, yellow perch, whatever—in its talons, it glided over the white village, scaling toward the river, the exact other way from the eagle.

And I think, today, how the bird went my way today, more or less exactly, a route down this ridge, then across the train rails right about here. Heavy-breathing anthropomorphism on my part, I know, but it still makes me shiver. Something auspicious in the coincidence of our routes, even if mine be earthbound? Maybe.

I've traveled these broken down tracks for a handful of minutes, a quarter mile or so. All the while I've been noticing the blackberries on my left side, and on the other, toward the river, the cow corn in Paul Knox's field. The berries are still a bit sour, but they are still as edible—I sample them as I pass—as the hard corn isn't, at least by mannish old me.

Enough of my squeamish and persnickety stalling, because at last I come on the mix of signs, in several senses, I appear to have wanted: in the middle of the tracks I spot a very monument of wild crap; it contains corn and berry and fish scale, and several sprigs of beaver hair quilled into it for good measure. The scat could be bear, but it's not; even this low, it could be bobcat, but it's not. It was shat by Coyote, the ever adaptable one, maybe even the brindled mutt who generously showed herself to me last May when I sat in my turkey blind.

I'd like to think so. In any case, as if offered permission, I squat, thinking—more wrongly than ever—that I too am an adaptable one.

Lord God, what a claim! Despite all the dreary romance that we silly reductivists, pro and con, have attached to him from the dawn of existence, Coyote is in the end the truly adaptable one, so obviously so that this latest anthropomorphic posturing of mine is nonsense in spades.

I seem to remain, well, full of it.

Did I just say reductivists? Yes. Because if you mention Coyote, one party's bound simply to glorify him, as if that were a real compliment or even relevant. I think of a book that, as I write this, decorates the best-seller lists: *Prodigal Summer*, by Barbara Kingsolver, an author so good and subtle elsewhere that her insipid inversion of the Big Bad Wolf tale in that novel simply baffles me.

The sentimentalists' allegedly anti-sentimental (but equally simplistic) adversaries will blame Coyote for every farm or ranch catastrophe (and for damn near every other rural misery), and will therefore demand his elimination. The tactics are mind-searing: cyanide, sniper helicopters, electrocution, on and on. They are also, I'm happy to note, invariably unsuccessful.

Life, human and otherwise, is too complex for both brands of crap, to use the noun of the hour, as it is for any simplism. I've learned that much if no more as poet and rambler. Unpersuaded by either of the parties I've just caricatured (both of which, I know personally, include people of intelligence, humanity, ecological conscience, the rest), I still conclude, inconclusively, that—well, I love Coyote. I love him for making every block thinker's stupidity so glaringly evident. I love him for that very trait of elusiveness, physical and metaphorical, the badge of his adaptability:

He is here now; there now; here again. And what do we observers make of that or this, or this or that? He's an animal who longs for red meat, but he'll eat a bug or a train-squashed berry, a roving chicken, a pickerel, an ear of cattle-corn, the worm that thrives on that corn, a maggot or marmot. Coyote likes woods and high plains and desert and mountain—but he'll raid an L.A. garbage can, if necessary, for the waste we dump into the world. He'll do anything, really, will go anywhere to keep ahead of us. As he has done, and does, and shall.

I do more than flatter myself also to imagine Coyote as my emblem animal on the mere grounds that we both long for wildness. My longing is qualitatively different from his: he's had to accommodate the assault of loud engines down here; I used to thrill—till the freights stopped running—to the cliff-muted whistle that's a ghost around me now, to the even ghostlier clack of steel wheels on these rails, bowed, exactly, around coyote poop, next to which I now make my wretched contribution.

Whether I make sense or nonsense, though, I'm stunned by my own happiness.

Bears again

THE CLIFF I DESCENDED A WHILE AGO EDGES CLOSE TO THE TRACKS AGAIN A few hundred yards on from the mess I so deliberately and presumptuously mixed with a wild thing's. It's even nearer to sheer vertical there, where, for reasons of fitness (and/or perversity), I decide to head back up.

Earlier on, I mentioned that I seem to court my own aloneness on these rambles. I should have mentioned that I do so in part for more or less practical reasons. The climb I'm starting will here and there be more or less dangerous. Not the Half Dome or whatever, but dicey enough. In the likeliest company I'd have, that of my wife, I wouldn't dare such a thing. There's a lot, large and petty, to this rambling business.

Within yards of the railbed, sticking straight into my face, growing out of the cliff-flank and parallel to the ground, there's a youngish apple tree. Its fruit's still mostly green, but it shows at least a suspicion of pink, the sort of thing that appeals to me in my occasional, fantastic self-portrait as hunter-gatherer: I can't say why, but I rather prefer sour apples to fully ripe.

Another rambling picker, a bear—less than full grown, I judge, by the height of its reach—has felt the same appeal, has eaten to surfeit, puked, then headed who knows where? Maybe already to den for the winter.

To den? Unlikely, but not out of the question. Speaking of sentimentality, your non-rambler may accept the common notion that weather is what drives a bear to lie down. But it's rather a matter of how much fat he or she has lodged under the hide as winter nears.

"Apples just keep the bear going," says David Tobey, expert among experts, like any of his streamlined hounds: "He needs something heartier than that to fatten him for sleep."

Dave's talking about mast: acorns if need be, beechnuts preferably. A good supply of such food means an early denning. A skinny supply means animals restless well into autumn, and more frequent human encounters as the animals come downhill to raid the landfill, the bird feeder, the pumpkin patch, and so on. Those encounters are routinely sensationalized, of course, even by old-timers who should (and probably do) know better: there hasn't been a fatal bear attack in Vermont, I believe, since the 19th century, when—incidentally—the big brutes were a good deal rarer than now. It's a very shy creature we're discussing, so much so that whenever I see one I feel graced by the heavens.

But as I was saying, plenty of mast means plenty of dormant bear even in September, though normally a little later than now to be sure. There aren't many beechnuts this year, as it happens, but such an abundance of acorns as to send you royally sprawling, should you traipse too casually across a windrow of them. (That's yet another odd peril I might have listed in "How To Be an Expert Rambler.") This fall, there are hills that the oaknuts have actually made unclimbable. So, despite the fact that at valley level, where the river-mist keeps things damp, and these vomitings therefore look pretty fresh, our young bear may just be snoozing even now, full of feed. Unusually early? No doubt; but I've known odder things.

If I've demonstrated anything thus far, it's that for me to think of one thing is shortly to connect it, however obliquely, to the next, and to the next and next and next. And to think of Bear just now means sooner or later both to leap ahead a season in mind and then many a season back.

It's an end of February in the early '60s, and Ray Hulett, postmaster of a town off west of here, summons me to climb a similar ridgeside. He won't tell me what our object is before we get to it. Stubborn, Ray all over. Which is quite a Ray.

There's been a major midwinter thaw, and it turns out that on the preceding evening, while Hulett was rambling himself, he came on a place where a fallen pine, massive through the bole, provided a front wall for a shallow cave, so that the pregnant sow could hunch there, hidden, snug when the snow came. She must have expected that snow to make a lean-to roof along the boughs, between rock above and trunk out front, and to fill in the branches of the wall as well. An igloo, more or less.

Her plan probably worked, but by the time Ray and I arrive, the recent melt has left her high and dry, her lone, tiny cub mewling, clinging, suckling. I'd like to claim that we're unarmed. I am, but Ray's not: he has a monstrous .45 pistol strapped to his sinewy thigh, just in case.

He tells me to pick up the cub, which has barely grown decent hair. Maybe, no surely, I shouldn't obey. But I do.

Ray whispers, "Smell of it."

Again I obey. (Don't ask me why, but Ray, skinny as a pipe-cleaner, is a man you take orders from.) Then he asks me, "Is that the woodsiest thing you ever *did* smell?"

I guess by God it is.

The whole episode takes no more than 30 seconds. I put the cub back on the comatose sow's belly, near as I dare to her abraded teats, and watch it squirm its way up to the nearest dug.

"You'd think he'd do better than hind tit," Ray jokes. "No competition and all."

Then he and I retreat, wordless. During our descent I conclude that this experience will surely—how could it otherwise?—remain one of a modest number to inhabit my imagination for a lifetime.

As indeed it does. I can smell that cub right here, clearly as I ever did there. Woodsy, all right.

Later Ray and I will fall out. He'll die after 20-odd following years in which we don't speak to each other, for all that he taught me, for all that I love and revere and resent him even in memory, that wiry, comic, bright, opinionated Yankee son of a bitch, for whom his way was forevermore the only way.

I can't even remember anything specific causing our rift, but it must have been nowhere near as important as it so long seemed, not to either of us. I do by heaven miss him.

So if it all comes together, one divagation upon another, one ramble after the next, even one big mistake after the next: how? How can all this ever produce a coherence? I ask you. I'm nothing if not serious.

❧

Beggar ticks

There's a skirt of low growth between the Macintosh tree and my first hard pull up the bank, which all too soon will become the cliff. (Why would I deliberately *look* for this sort of effort, as Tink would surely ask, as I'm shortly bound to ask myself a time or two?). Having bulled through that growth, I discover that it contains a colony of beggar ticks, little viper-headed burrs that grab onto every moving wild thing within their ken. They cling just the same to a human thing like me, with its rag socks, its ripped jeans, its trail-weary sweatshirt, its leghairs—I'm just another passing beast, one with nothing but welcoming surfaces.

The burrs are so profuse I won't even guess at their numbers; they're peppered over every inch of leg and clothing, mid-thigh to boot-lace.

Profanely as possible, I wish each last little one of the graspy bastards in hell (where I'll be picking them, no doubt, for my sins). Then I calm down, resigned already to an agonizingly long spell of sitting and plucking at home—because I'll be damned and Goddamned if I'll sow these riders along my rambler's journey, which is how they beg to be broadcast. No,

Mister Man, I'll send every last son of a whore of them down our hypercivilized, state-of-the-art toilet, wildness be damned.

Struggling, I rise to about 300 feet over the tracks, when to my surprise I come on another flat interval sopping with beaverwork, this one twice as large and twice as active as the one I passed earlier in the hour. Never mind that one: if the water-seekers had found *this* place.... Each vein and fissure in the schist fairly pours.

It pours into the very sort of cedar swamp I looked for yesterday. This is the least likely spot for that I could have imagined. And yet it's a swamp right enough, no matter that it's been wrought by mammals more than by geology, and that the cedars themselves grow pretty puny nearby. Or rather, the ones the beavers have left upright do. Not that the other cedars, mere stubs now, have actually been eaten. Why would the beavers bother, with those succulent popple whips on the far side? No, they used the evergreens' lacy branches to bind their more than usually clever dam; I can see them matted into its fabric. By God, these famously busy engineers were determined, for whatever earthly reason, to make a cliffside lodge! They meant to set up, not simply pass through, and so they did. Why choose so strange a spot for that? They must know; I don't.

There are other strangenesses here, though none as deep as that one. I'm surprised for one thing by how much farther north I've come than I guessed, much farther along this particular palisade, in fact, than I've ever been till now on foot. I must have mused my way up the tracks for a lot more minutes than I'd thought.

I'm also surprised by a reverie (what's new?), and by the fact that it comes to me here rather than down there where the rail traffic used to pass. It's the cedar-ness of where I stand that prompts it, I'm sure, never mind that each last tie I stepped on along the tracks was of the same lumber.

Cedars.

I recall George MacArthur's accounts of making railway ties, or "sleepers" as they were called, on White's Island in the winter of 1927. He lodged as a lone wolf in a small shack—cedar too—on the shore of the icebound lake. He never saw that building by daylight in the three months he lived out there that season.

"Up with a lantern to work, back with it when I got done."

It was all piece-work, not salaried. You were paid by the sleeper, 25¢ for an A-quality, 15¢ for a B. You lugged a lot of gear, in a packbasket and by hand: the lighter axe and saw for swamping out a place, so your cedar wouldn't hang up in the canopy when you felled it; same tools for topping and limbing; the spud for debarking your log; the crosscut for reducing your stick to four-foot bolts; the peavey to roll your bolts into hewing position; wedges; sharpening stones; spare blades; a lunchpail; a galvy water jug; matches to kindle a fire to thaw the jug when you were thirsty.

Then the sleeper axe itself, more or less resembling the axes you see in heraldry: 16 pounds, short-handled, a blade 14 inches along the bit. After the swamping and peeling and bunking, you stood on the fallen trunk section itself; then, using the edge of your gumboot as a guide, you swung that monster and shaved a flat face.

"And there was your sleeper," George said, as if the hewn tie were no more difficult to produce than a whittled poke-stick. "I turned out 34 of 'em in a day one time," George boasted. "I hewed the rubber off'n a bunch of boots too, but I never cut myself."

Next morning at some point, the teamster would come by to load the ties and make a count for the company's purser. So George would have hefted all those sleepers out of the wetland the night before, too, up to the sledge-trail.

Hearing all this for the first time, I got righteous: I called the whole arrangement a corruption. Why, it paid George $18 in his best week! It was a clear instance of moneyed interests exploiting the labor of the unmoneyed.

To my surprise, George objected: "You took pride in your work! I was the best hand they was, and everybody knew it. Never felt better, and I made up all them poems of mine, and that-like."

The poems were all more or less alike, though each was in its way a work of genius. Iambic tetrameter, mostly couplets, each line barbed with irony toward an occasion or person. For example, the long one aimed at the out of state crew sent by the WPA to supervise the locals as they built the town schoolhouse in the '30s:

Now friends, you know it's been quite a time
Since I been here to say a rhyme.
But I'm going to give this one to you
If I don't get killed before I'm through.
The other night I had a dream
Of a schoolhouse built in Grand Lake Stream.
They built that school in our little town
For seventeen thousand dollars,
And I can't see why they'd build a barn
For educating scholars.

The poem was recited, like all of George's poems and stories, in an interval between skits in the town hall, where townsfolk put on their own minstrel shows for community entertainment. The boss of the supervisory crew was on hand, and he saw to it that George was fired the very next day.

"I was happy enough for that anyhow," he told me. "I belonged in the woods, and back I went."

Well, for all his pride in his woodsmanship, I'm still right: George was exploited. I'm just not *entirely* right. What's new?

There were, of course, hardships in tie-making jobs George did all through the era that preceded chainsaws and skidders. He wouldn't go so far as to deny that. He told me of snowshoeing across the lake and then five miles homeward every Sunday in that winter of '27, to visit his wife and family in town through the short daylight hours, then into camp again at dusk. He remembered one hike back to that sorry shack after sunset, the snow so heavy he cut a pole to wallop it out of his shoes every third step, and still it stuck like gumbo. He sweated, hard, and the sweat froze up on his body.

"It run down between my back-end cheeks," he said, dryly. "Iced up and chafed some. Had to hold myself apart for the last two miles and over the lake."

Then up and at it at false dawn. Work, I imagine, that would kill a lot of men in our own time.

Because I'd listened so often to George's real-life tales, you can guess what I thought some years later when, boy professor at Dartmouth, my first job, I watched an autumn throng of students unload a truckload of those hard-hewn sleepers, which they piled into a tower. Then they burnt the whole mess to ash the next evening, chanting "Beat Harvard" or whatever. At least four weeks' effort in that pile for Uncle George in '27, or for someone like him.

I felt a mix of rage and sadness then, as I do again on this trackless sidehill, even though I'm sure I was just as blithe about the world of hard work and valor and endurance at those college kids' age. Maybe I show something like blitheness even now, without even knowing how or why or when or where or toward whom.

And somehow I imagine that the aloneness of George's brutal work was a part of his pleasure, or at least of his contemplation. It seems—no, it is—pretentious to compare the aloneness and the physical effort I experience on a ramble, even up a stiff sidehill like this one here, to George as he swung that killer axe. It's only that I know, or think I know, how a certain aloneness is so deep in you when you are feeling it that the only way to make sense of it is to call it good.

He'll never leave my mind's eye, George. He lives out there on an island I know, though the island is all changed now, and he's still hewing cedar ties, true enough for a straight-edge, in a winter that preceded my own winter birth by 15 years. He's a figure of resolution, he's a spirit, he's a dynamo, he's a speck amid the miles and miles of iced-over lake around him, onto which falls the pure powder of 20-below-zero evening, and he's still working in that showering by the last of the short day's light.

***

Over the dam

I'M NO BEAVER EXPERT, BUT EVEN IF I SEE NONE AT THIS HOUR, I KNOW that these ones are still living way up here. I can't be certain exactly how long they've been here, but a pretty long time, I'd judge, by the look of the surrounding popples, small fodder patch by now mostly reduced to stakes, so that the animals' paths range farther and farther from the lodges (there are two). Dangerous stuff: the cat and the coyote and the fisher must be happy to see them stray. I cast about for signs of predator kills, but come up empty.

The beavers have been here long enough anyway, I discover, that my progress over their dam becomes a seriously demanding affair: all manner of cattails explode in my face, and grasses and steeplebush have grown high all along the apron. Worse, here and there I also confront a barrier of red osier, which natives call "witch-hobble," tougher by far to negotiate than any other brush, tougher than the steepness below, or the further steepness that awaits me.

I'll let that steepness go on waiting for the moment. After thrashing my way across the beaver dam, through its vegetation, into its flowage and out, I flop against the sidehill, puffed out, wet with sweat and turd-tinted water. I must rest.

Now I don't much like rest. Somehow it mildly depresses me, and so even can sleep: when I'm unconscious or stationary like that, I know too damn many things are going on elsewhere, without me. I don't need much bedtime, luckily; last night's five hours were plenty, and I was pleased that a fox-bark, right below my window, woke me at 5:15. I sneaked down the stairs; what a pleasure to envision the tour I'm now recording.

Odd duck.

Even in the Ticino, some later while from this morning, no foxbark anywhere nearby, the dark lingering till after seven o'clock in the early winter, I'll be up way earlier. I'll step outside, where nothing is visible but stars, but where, I dream, I'm at least ready for... something.

I finally stand and move, I breathe hard climbing, I blow a moment or two at height of land.

The rest, however, is easy. I follow a well worn twitch road south. Thirty downhill minutes and I'm home. ꩜.

home

Home: names and lists and tales

HOME. THE VERY WORD IS SO GIGANTIC IN ITS IMPLICATIONS, FOR ANYONE, that I won't dwell on it too long. Like memories of childhood, of mother, father, grandparents, siblings, cousins—on and on—the subject belongs not in another book, one other book, but in all the books a man might write in a lifetime.

As of course it does in my case. Nothing I've ever composed, I'm convinced, lacks influences from—"home." (*In the Ticino, I'll remember how odd it is that Italian, language of family obsession, has no equivalent word.*) Often, traveling professionally, larking on a hunting or fishing trip somewhere, above all rambling, I'll actually pause now and then to recite to myself the name of my wife, "Robin," and then, in descending order of age, the names of my children: "Creston." "Erika." These from a prior marriage. "Jordan." "Catherine." "Sydney." These with Robin.

The guttering of my first marriage is a painful thing to acknowledge. The failure was almost entirely mine, and even after more than 20 years I brood on that, brood on that breach of vows. I'd not undo that part of my life, if only because to do that would be to undo those two older children, whose talents and above all whose decencies daily astound me. In their childhood years, their mother and I split their upbringing, one week here and one there, and colluded pretty well on that score, if I say so. I shall be forever grateful that my first wife has never in our relationship used, or even tried to use, the kids as pawns, even in those bitter early years of separation.

But I'm rather private about my family life, for reasons that are surely not altogether noble, though they have, I trust, their own decency too.

I have no right, I think, to drag them into my own written meditations without their contributions or rebuttals or affirmations. And, in all candor, there are things about myself that I don't say in public, unless it be to those closest to me on earth. And there's also this: to write appropriately on all these scores just seems beyond me, too hard. It's a want of talent, not of courage alone, that moves me here instead to talk about that list-making habit of mine.

If I start listing in the woods, I do the same at home—more there, in fact, than anywhere for some reason. Only to say certain names produces in me such a welter of associations, hopes, memories, fears, expectations, and disappointments (usually in myself, as I've just implied) that I pale at the prospect of saying much about what I feel. I'd sooner try to chart the whole of New England with a pocket compass and a chalkline than take on so unimaginably difficult an enterprise as "comment" on any of the people they stand for.

So I say the names again, naming having its own magic, as Adam amply demonstrated. The grass became grass, the rock rock, the centipede the centipede, once he'd said so. To name my family is to call it into presence even when it's not There.

Same thing, in a way, come to think of it, when Uncle George MacArthur and his brother Franklin named Dawn Marie Beach on Wabassus Lake for a local mixed-blood child; in the naming, the beach became itself. Once in winter my wife and I saw a horde of flying squirrels sail out of a rotting white pine and all the way down a long sidehill; the place became for us The Flying Squirrels, and so became always availably real. The Water Lot was at one time no more than a spongy piece of earth over ledge; in fact it still is—but it's the Water Lot and nothing else forever. On and on.

One of the things that most satisfies me about all my children, a thing that in fact plain thrills me, is that each seems profoundly and genuinely to appreciate the sorts of places and people I do. All this name stuff is familiar turf, then. And I imagine them, even the youngest, reading another list of names I'm about to draw up and getting it.

Getting what? They know, even if I don't. I put lists together at home more than elsewhere because the flesh and spirit of so much gregarious kin beside me or nearby or even in mind moves me that way. I may be lazing, half-awake (at best) after a ramble, in the recliner the family gave me six years ago, when I cut myself to the legbone with a chainsaw. The woodstove is humping; snow sifts down outside; the dogs woof in slumber, limbs twitching, hot after fantasy game; someone is humming a silly old pop tune.

Or I may be washing a dish or scaring up a supper, autumn's light a wonder against the kitchenside ridge.

Or I may be smoking a cigar on the porch, looking down on the pond, where swallows prowl the dusk for food. (There used to be nighthawks, with their glorious *boom* of wing, but no more: I keep harking back to that loss.) Emerald newts embrace on the pond. Spring has arrived, its lilac odors sneaking in the open windows, the grey frogs trading notes.

I may be back from a summertime trout-float on the upper Connecticut, too arm-weary from rowing and casting and too peaceful even to change my clothes, back in the recliner. A doe barks at her wandering fawn. A barred owl trades notes with another. Bats flit across a cuticle moon.

And on this Friday evening in September, the gentle rains have come in, and my list is all names again, old Yankee names for various wild things. I compose it, then wonder if each soubriquet isn't just as accurate as any Latin one. There's a European bird, say, called a yellowhammer; if folks hereabouts use the same name for the yellow-shafted flicker, an altogether different species, is the flicker any less what he is? The people who name it yellowhammer all know which creature they refer to, don't they? Oh, the question could get too thorny; I'll content myself with the nicknames' collective resonance:

Brush Wolf, the coyote.
Gorby (or *Whiskeyjack* or *Camprobber* or *Moosebird*), the gray jay.
Injun Devil, the fisher.
Chiplifter, the staghorn beetle.
No-see-um, the biting midge.
Little Dipper, the grebe.
Bullbane, the witch hazel.
Fool Hen, the (rare) spruce grouse.

Coony Rabbit, the (vanished) cottontail.
Beetbird, the goldfinch.
Hedgehog, the porcupine.
Devil's Needle, the damselfly.
Sheldrake, the redbreasted merganser.
Blue Darter, the sharpshinned hawk.
Thorn Plum, the hawthorn.
Ivory Plum, the whatever-it-is.
Wet Dog, the trillium.
Leverwood, the hop hornbeam.
Hackmatack, the larch.
Bellbird, the hermit thrush.
Calling the Wind, the loon's slower cry.

The names make a poem, at least in my ears, whatever their order.

Names can make a spell as I muse at home. But home is also where name-full anecdotes like certain ones in these pages find their best audience too, just as, I hope, I'm audience for others' yarns here. The ones about Tink and the St. Bernard, Ray Hulett and the bear cub, Uncle George on White's Island: my wife, my kids know them, and what they mean.

They also know the one that comes to me now, some smell of hot oil on the stove perhaps calling it up, about Dolly Campbell, whom I went to see after her husband Zane died.

Dolly's a doughnut maker, an artist, famed for it. Zane and their three daughters admired her goodies so much they urged her to cook for the family's store. Later, after she and Zane sold that place, she branched out, delivering doughnuts on both sides of the Connecticut. She and Zane added a roomy kitchen on the backside of their trailer, where I found Dolly when I came by on my sympathy call.

Zane's dog Bianca moped in a corner. ("Heinz's 57 Varieties," Zane used to say of her breeding.) She clearly felt depressed by her owner's vanishing: there was never any doubt that Bianca was Zane's companion and no one else's. Dolly, rushing from one boiling kettle to another and another, still kept up her end of the talk, very cheerily in fact. That's a good, bright, brave woman.

Half tripping at one point over Bianca, she recalled how, after he retired, Zane liked to harvest doughnut holes from Dolly's morning batch, then sit on the sofa and share them with his dog, the pair of them carelessly watching "The Price Is Right."

She and I laughed out loud together at her memory. By the Jesus, that Zane! My eyes clouded a bit, but tears from Dolly's dropped into the hot grease, where they danced and spat.

"Well, *they're* lively anyhow!" Dolly said, and, if such a thing is possible, she giggled valiantly. Alone now, but keeping on, God bless her.

Yes, my family knows that anecdote.

Families, it seems to me, are fragile as wildness; indeed, they possess a kind of wildness themselves, with luck a largely benign kind like the other, though never exclusively so. In any case, they're forever, I trust. It takes some courage.

Just like home, at least in mind.

a saturday

Tocc' al ferro

THE RAMBLING ITCH IS PRACTICALLY NONEXISTENT THIS MORNING. THE body doesn't cotton to the mind's intentions. Or is that the other way round? It doesn't matter. The point is I'd as soon have stood in bed, as Tink would put it; I plain don't want to carry out today's project—or any project. Not in this kind of pain.

I came out of sleep with a familiar throb in my right hip—not arthritic, the doctors insist, but it sure feels that way. Hope not.

Tocc' al ferro, they say in Italian: *Touch iron*, not wood, for good luck.

Thank heavens something changes my balky mind (crow-call? hen turkey-yelp? small tumble of water out of the pond?). I grab a bowed ski pole. *Tocc' al ferro*, I whisper, mouth too dry to roll the *r* properly.

What I touch is not iron, of course, but at least it's metal. The ski pole may not bring luck, but it'll do at least to help me up the ridge just behind my study shack, 200 yards from the house, where, on a weekend, my wife and younger children still sleep, she briefly free of professional work, they of school. Once more I realize that I'm lucky as it is.

I've brought along a pole like this since 1975, the year I decided I wouldn't ever use it again for its designed purpose, because the ski industry had already done so much to wreck the wildness I hoped to cherish till I was gone, or the wildness was. I've toted it, that is, since well before I knew the Italian version of Touch Wood, and I'd recommend a similar staff, whatever its physical properties, to every rambler on the planet.

Just now I'm trying hard not to think of it as a crutch or cane, though of course it is. And yet, I assure myself, it's one I've been using for much of my rambling life, and for all sorts of good reasons:

A staff like that proves handy, for example, when you want to whack a bough, which—after something last night that wasn't quite snow nor rain—glitters and sags with frozen beads. That ice may prove the tree's ruin.

How often beauty marries ruin, I maunder: the time-ravaged colosseums of Rome or Verona are likely more beautiful today, at least to sentimental eyes like mine, than they were in their glory; I've seen East Coast sunrises that were almost Turneresque in their shapes and hues—thanks to the smog drifting offshore from Megalopolis, drifting all over God's earth. Venice's skies under the haze from Maestre's factories may be more Tintorettish now than they were in the painter's own era.

Will I show anything like grace, let alone beauty, in my own ruin? It's a question I seem to ask more and more, moved to it by this damned hip or some other ache, even though the hip's feeling a lot less shaky now that I'm up and around and getting ready to go.

As I was saying, the rambler's staff can save a tree by ridding it of its ice-weight, even if one's real intention was to unsag the limbs, to clear an upright passage to walk under. But more often, there's the simple matter of keeping your feet on a steep slope, whether you're headed up or down. I was glad, yesterday, to have this warped pole as I crossed that strange beaver pond and climbed the ridge above it; and I'll be glad again to use it this morning.

You can mount the pole to your shoulder, if that's your instinct, like mine, when you flush a gamebird or kick a whitetail out of bed. Then you can swing it like a gun while you reconstruct certain scenes in your head—the whirr of a grouse down a narrow gap in the canopy, here and gone, or a gaggle of early teal, just visible over the river as the dawn smears the marsh reeds with an ochre brush, or a woodcock spiraling upward through the pale-leafed aspens.

I've even used my ski pole like a jouster's lance, to fend off a nasty dog, who seemed—what nerve!—to consider his wandering as valuable as my own. The mutt's breeding included a heavy, feisty dose of Chow: I noted those Asian eyes; but there was something else in the mix too that gave him 90-plus pounds of bulk, enough to make me happy for my crude weapon, though I don't mean to over-dramatize: this mongrel had made a half-serious charge, yes, no wag of tail; I made a full-serious lunge at his chest, drawing a jot of blood—which settled things, at least temporarily. The dog ran off. Or rather he ambled away, not quite humiliated, and maybe not done with the nervous likes of me.

But I began by recalling my own resistance to the climb I'd planned, as sharp as yesterday's. I'll have to learn more and more about how to deal with such resistance, how to plan counter-resistance. I've been what they call Type A all my life, but I'm close to 60 now and I'll need to develop Type B behavior, along with some other gratification than muscle contraction, if I want to keep pushing along in whatever fashion.

Ramble as poem (reprise)

Other gratification? How about writing? So you may ask on my behalf. Yes, that can work, though in my career writing has often felt oddly like muscular exertion itself. Especially poetry, which especially responds to and even bases itself on a kind of rambler's itchiness. Maybe even in these pages I'm looking for a sort of meditation that springs out of different sources from all the ones I'm used to, that doesn't so much resemble physical exercise.

I haven't much hope I'll make such a change, at least not for a while: that is, if I'm really looking to do so at all. Truth to tell, now that my hip's stopped throbbing, my failure seems fine by me. Fine, now that I'm outdoors, now that I'm moving. I've got to walk, I've got to row, I've got to paddle, I've got to hunt, I've got to fish. I've got to do something, for God's sake! I can't just sit here, even if writing this or anything obviously means that I must.

But it's not really a stationary thing at all. Which is hard to explain. Obviously.

Onward and/or backward

The serious portion of this Saturday ramble starts with a push through the brambled wreckage of a burn, which stands between me and my intended ascent. The berrycanes' barbs inscribe themselves on my hands and forearms and—despite heavy trousers—my leg. All worth it. I'm even slightly vain of these blood tattoos.

Winter's not far off, and when it rushes in, the bramble patch will make good cover for voles, small rodents who tunnel under the snow, making mazes to astound you when the melt comes and you find them in the dingy grass of earliest spring. The thorns will be of some help in discouraging their predators, fox and bobcat and coyote and ermine. I like to see those predator's tracks in the cold months, especially the cat's: how *busy* they make him look, treading around and into and out of the briar stand, here and there making a quick cuff mark in the snow. You wonder if he came up empty or with a pathetic little wiggler stuck on a talon.

But I like the in-line tracks of the fox, too, the dog print of the coyote, and those little paired punctures of the hopping weasel, neat as the white animal himself. It's all a kind of wonderful writing, as wonderful in its way as anyone's.

At the far side of the briars, I study a route to the crest. While I do so, I find myself standing by a certain timber ramp, which has all but moldered into absence by now. I've seen this ramp and others like it, a hundred times, all over the local country. You come on them especially at the bases of hills like this one and along water banks.

They're only so many logs stacked in a grid, with a couple of longer rounds on the top leaning toward whatever track or sluice passes conveniently by. There are old-timers who'll tell you that the top logs always point toward water, that they can therefore straighten you out when you've got twisted around in the woods; the old folks may be right—except that everything on earth can be said to point at water sooner or later.

Anyhow, the loggers of another day loaded their wagons and sledges by hefting and cant-dogging their lumber onto the ramp, then rolling it down to some sort of waiting conveyance—sledge, wagon, water itself. Of course, this is all from way back before my time. The ramps, which as a younger man I saw in their original sturdiness, have pretty much vanished.

Yes, in my own little memory they were as common as the now dwindled fish hawks. My first reaction to their disappearance this morning is a self-rebuke: I should have caught on to all this evanescence a long time ago. I think about the passage of my personal span, of course, but when I get over that knee-jerk self-indulgence I start thinking (the Wordsworth instinct again) about the loggers themselves: the ones who used these structures are even longer gone than the ramp they fashioned next to me here, one through whose ghostliness and debris are poking everything from Joe Pye Weed to two slim, rather girlish aspens, 30 feet tall if an inch.

I spoke of Dolly, but to stand in this spot is to think of her husband Zane, whose left leg was once pinned by a long log spilt from one of these ramps. So he walked with a colorful limp till the day he died, just a week ago. When I say "colorful," I mean that his walk resembled one I saw as a child, well before I ever knew Zane himself; it belonged to the John Wayne character in "The High and the Mighty."

Back then I was innocent of Wayne's blockhead-mean, McCarthyite politics, and wouldn't have known what to make of them anyhow. All I cared for was how distinctive it looked, the stiff leg he kept swinging around in that movie. And so it was that I tried the same walk out at school, explaining in my pathetic, baldface-lying way that I'd been thrown from my horse—a fat hay-burner Shetland mix named Miss Prim, in fact, whom I practically had to whip bloody to get lazily trotting.

I'd turn my back on my classmates, gaze out the window stoically, explain that I'd never walk normally again.

As I said somewhere above, I hope it's okay to have once been young and stupid.

I was full of other cockamamie stunts in those young days. Once, for example, on some wild whim I bought an eye patch at Streeper's, the neighborhood drugstore. The shop window still displayed those tall vials, which were archaic even then, full of inscrutable amber and violet liquids. I wonder when I stopped seeing those in pharmacy windows. One day they just weren't there anymore—like these lumber ramps.

The eye patch was too much, as even I knew, for school. Still I put it on after, went as so often to the Grove Diner, ordered the same chicken salad sandwich as always from Louie the counterman, who knew me and my tastes like his palm.

I used a French-ish accent, which I'd borrowed from that crooked police captain in "Casablanca": "One cheeken sand-weedge, *s'il vous plâit*," said I.

Louie didn't seem to pay me any mind, so I upped the ante: "You can call me 'Frenchy,'" I said, pronouncing it *Franchy*.

"All *right*!" Louie shouted to Eb the fry-cook, and when I saw his sneer, I knew my jinx was already up: "One chicken salad san'ich… for *Franchy*!"

Then the bastard turned back to me, very slowly. "*Haw. Haw. Haw*," he said, also very slowly, articulating each monosyllable, the bastard.

I ripped off the patch, gloomy with embarrassment.

The bastard.

I guess I've somehow always wanted to be a character, and hoped someone would call me that on my funeral day. On Zane's day, the first words in the preacher's eulogy simply couldn't have been other than the covetable ones: "Zane Campbell was a character!"

Zane, an interlude

HOWEVER EXPECTED, THE MINISTER'S SENTENCE AROUSED LAUGHTER FROM all the many assembled in that north-country marble orchard. We knew the man.

God bless him now.

Zane's education had been minimal. We knew that, knew too that he therefore took a special pride in the copious vocabulary he developed on his own. He'd seen action in World War II, and afterwards became a zealous historian of the European campaign; he read widely on a lot of subjects, but on that one he was downright erudite. Several of us were present in his general store one afternoon, for example, to hear him correct a Dartmouth history professor's remark on some battle unknown to any among us but the prof—and Zane.

This entire book would be worth the time I've put into it if I could just bring the sound of Zane Campbell's voice to life: cigarette-hoarsened, but rumbling and orotund. I could listen to it for hours on end right now, the way I used to.

It was quite a few years after his logging accident that Zane and Dolly bought their store. The crowds flocked in, not only because the couple ran it so competently but also because you never left the place without hearing some fanciful anecdote or some actual history or both—always colorful stuff.

Zane sold Christmas trees in the holiday season, nice trees at that, and come December he'd constantly be after me to buy one. But I've always been a nostalgist, I guess, so I insisted on cutting ours from the back woodlot, where the spruce grew not so bushy nor beautiful, no, but abundant.

One year I'd been on the road for a spell, Christmas was three days off, and I finally thought of caving in to Zane; but at the last moment I once again twitted him about his big prices, and told him I'd get my own tree before the 25th, same as usual.

I woke on the 23rd to find a perfectly rounded fir balsam in my driveway. Assuming, of course, that because it was too late to sell anything out of his remainder stock, Zane had delivered it at night, I went to thank him.

"'Twa'n't *me*," he rasped.

From then on for years, right up till Zane and Dolly retired, I'd get the same present—sometimes as many as three trees, in fact—just before Christmas. But the storekeeper always claimed he had "no notion of their provenance" or some such highfalutin stuff. His deadpan was worthy of a Keaton, so over time, I got so I believed him.

I was disabused on the day the Campbells were packing the last of their personal effects from the upstairs apartment.

"Won't get no more free trees," Zane commented when I stopped to lend what hand I could. His comment, as the locals say, was dryer than a popcorn fart.

"You mean you *have* been dropping them off all this time?"

"'Course."

"You had me fooled."

"Not hard," Zane replied. (He pronounced the latter word like *had*).

"How'd it start?" (I tried on stat for size; he eyed me skeptically: I hadn't succeeded.)

"Waall, you were by one evenin' and wouldn't buy one, so I dispatched

Stevie Balch on that errand, told him to deposit one at your place after we got done with poker later along... *in my mobile home*, no less!"

"Zane," I asked, "was John Barleycorn a part of all this?"

"Waall," Zane answered, deadpan still, but with that fabulous voice and intonation, "he was implicated at the start." (*Stat* worked fine for him.)

Another confession, a nice distinction.

Having gotten this far in my written rambles, I'll briefly leave the Ticino to visit an Italian friend. Somewhere in Lugano or Milan or in train or taxi or streetcar, I will mislay the notes I'd transcribed from my tape recorder back in the States.

Frantic, I'll call the Italian and Swiss transport authorities, then the restaurant in which my wife, one of our children, our Italian chum and I will have taken our lunch, then the custodian at the Palazzo Liberty, where we'd heard a magnificent all-Mozart program by the Chamber Orchestra of Milan.

Nothing.

Back home, hoping I never brought the notes along at all, I'll ransack our rented house, my classroom and office at the university, its library, even its lavatories. I'll query the staff, from grounds keeper to president.

Nothing.

I'll even repeat a vulgar prayer to St. Anthony, over and over, on the advice of a local American friend:

St. Anthony, St. Anthony! Please come around.
My papers are missing and need to be found.

For a few days, to continue work on this book will seem unthinkable. I'd begun it in the spirit of accuracy and honesty, and—my memory not what it was, the notes recorded six months back—I won't bring myself to lie about my second rambling day, which I'd scarcely begun to render when I left for the ill-starred trip. Now everything must stop dead.

I won't merely pick and choose things and events that I might have witnessed on that Saturday and present them as actual experience. I could do so, to be sure, given all my past wanderings among the local hills and woods, but somehow that that would rob the writing's savor, for me and readers both. Or so I'll conclude.

I will, to euphemize, be deeply dejected.

And then one morning it will dawn on me that what I'd already written consisted as much of inward travel as outward, indeed more. In a sense, physical situations had been my goad to non-physical reflection right along. (Consider for instance the phantom buck I "saw" from that rock-seat of mine in a deadfall blind.) What I observe in the palpable world and what's inside, the physical and the visionary, and what these have to do with one another: that's always been my province, in this book and elsewhere. Indeed, the distinction between physical and—forgive me again—spiritual will strike me as more than ever impoverished, inexact.

Right along I've been showing my arrival at certain places and my subsequent movement downward into myself, upward into imagination's territory, outward, or wherever, toward the spiritual—rambling's seepage into my soul. Now I will reverse the process (as if that were a calculable option, as if the preceding process had truly been so neat).

My new departure will in fact be scarcely a departure at all.

In a word, I'll decide to make virtue of necessity. Having lost my notes, I'll have to imagine the day in question. That will enable me, among other things, and perhaps more than the notes would have, more thoroughly to explore the kinship between rambling and writing... though "writing" is never merely the recording of words on a page. Like rambling, it seems to stand for many things, some all but unfetchable.

Writing, rambling. Is either one thus a "metaphor for life"? I couldn't make that assertion in those terms exactly, not without more self-consciousness than I can bear. And who lives, who would want to, a purely metaphorical existence?

Rambling and writing (reprise)

I INDICATED AS EARLY AS I COULD THAT THE TRUE RAMBLER BEGINS WITHout a foreordained accomplishment in mind, even without any physical goal other than returning to where he started—ideally, in Eliot's phrase, to know the place for the first time. Or, in my amendment, to know it for one first time of the many apparent firsts to come.

Lost in the woods, the rambler uses lostness as a way to discover new territory or, a variation of the same thing, he approaches old territory from so unfamiliar a perspective that it might as well be new. In either case, there is an ineffable feeling, almost like a magnetic attraction, that moves him along in a certain direction or arc; the attraction can prove misleading, if there is such a thing on a ramble—he can be going exactly against the way he's surmised, but how is that a bad thing?

This is not Alaska or Brazil. No one's going to get too dangerously lost, unless he's in the remoter White or Green Mountains, as I'm generally not in these hikes. Let us see what we can see: my motto; the us is myself and my self.

My rambles are not allegorical until I make them that, which I'm more than reluctant to do. And yet, bewildered in the little wildness of my physical neighborhood—or "turned around," as the old-timers say, perhaps a bit embarrassed to have lost bearings in the first place—I'll begin to look for skyline, water-course, even the mossy north-side wanes of trees, and will in time come on something to set me straight. Signs.

Deprived of author's notes, however sketchy and impressionistic, I'll resort to similar groping, in the faith that imagination can make things whole, if only for a spell. I won't quite know where I'm going, and I'll take advantage of that, rambling on, yes, seeing what I see, yes, and making of it what I'm able. In such a manner, I'll find my guiding signs, if I find them at all, in mind.

My second day in mind

On day two, dawn shot up clear. The rains of the prior night had dried as a high pressure front swooped down from Canada. Our meadow was frosted so perfectly white that I hesitated to walk across it. My strides would leave great cumbrous Vs in the cover, a sloppy script at best. This much I recall without benefit of imagination, powerful, "awful" or otherwise.

Last evening, I fetched a volume of Coleridge's major works from the college library, because, hearing of my circumstances—however remotely akin to Coleridge's—my bosom friend in the Ticino, the poet Christopher Matthews, recommended that I consider "This Lime-Tree Bower My Prison."

Things come together, all right: Christopher from Brighton in south England, I from Newbury in central Vermont, and this year, by pure chance (or is it?), we share an office in Italian Switzerland, where we also share counsel and fellowship of an extraordinary kind. I shall miss him painfully when we leave. Lo and behold, Chris's recommendation of the Coleridge poem perfectly speaks to my soul's longing to conclude these ramblings appropriately. There are no coincidences, I sometimes believe.

In his headnote, the poet mentions an accident that kept him from a long walk with Charles Lamb and some others through countryside near Nether Stowey. (Coleridge's wife had in fact spilled hot food on his foot, proving that even the most exalted of bards lives in the same world we do—a comforting notion, if I think about it.)

The poem begins:

Well, they are gone, and here must I remain,
This lime-tree bower my prison! I have lost
Beauties and feelings, such as would have been
Most sweet to my remembrance even when age
Had dimmed mine eyes to blindness!

The speaker's only choice, which must contain something both of pain and uplift, is to imagine his would-be companions' progress through beloved territory:

> *... Now my friends emerge*
> *Beneath the wide wide Heaven—and view again*
> *The many-steepled tract magnificent*
> *Of hilly fields and meadows, and the sea....*

In my own case, the friends I imagine are ones who've appeared already in these meditations; but, aloneness being crucial to a real ramble, as opposed to an outing, they also and inevitably include myself. Indeed, they are only myself, about whom—in a different place and age—I could speak more or less as Coleridge speaks of Lamb:

> *... So my Friend*
> *Struck with deep joy may stand, as I have stood,*
> *Silent with swimming sense; yea, gazing round*
> *On the wide landscape, gaze till all doth seem*
> *Less gross than bodily; and of such hues*
> *As veil the Almighty Spirit, when yet he makes*
> *Spirits perceive his presence.*

The author has been there, clearly enough, in body—many times in fact; now, he is there in mind, and will "view again" a landscape as new and transporting as it ever was familiar.

In this book, I've also made a number of too coy references to the spirit. Yet the subject has remained both so immense and so private that I've been shy of facing it head-on. I'm still shy here. I'll claim only that by way of imagination, though that's too loose a term, some Spirit does seem now and then to make of me a spirit too, as in the last two lines just quoted.

This happens writing or rambling or both, just as it did for Coleridge, even when his longed for landscape lay so apparently far from his garden, among the "imprisoning" lime trees.

Scarcely imprisoned, I sit in our own rented garden this morning. No lime trees, but camellias, marguerites, the promise of roses all around. I find myself praying—maybe not the accurate term either—that there's some strength and accuracy in the images I present as I close, and in

ones I've presented earlier. I know they won't rival Coleridge's, but at least they'll borrow a share of the animus from "This Lime-Tree Bower" as it draws to its own close:

> ***My gentle-hearted Charles! when the last rook***
> ***Beat its straight path along the dusky air***
> ***Homewards, I blest it! deeming, its black wing***
> ***(Now a dim speck, now vanishing in light)***
> ***Had crossed the mighty orb's dilated glory....***

I'm a little ahead of myself, hardly for the first time.

I meant, as the saying goes, to make a day of that second day's ramble. My family would be away for most of it, my wife at a conference, our kids at friends' houses till late afternoon on a Saturday. I'd leave as the sun shot from the eastern ridge, and, daylight hours shrinking toward winter by now, would come back as it balanced momentarily on the western one: I expected dawn to be musical with birds despite the chill, and dusk to fill with crows, loudly plowing air from the Connecticut valley fields to their roosting stages just north, in numbers enough to thrill and stupefy me both.

For as long as time and visibility allowed, I'd head north as usual too, at first following a rough track between the Old County Road on my left and the river on my right. Maybe, in my northering, I'd stumble onto signs of the vanished farm settlement up that way, which Tink had often told me about, remembering talk of it from his childhood, when it was already little more than a rumor.

How old, then, would this ghost farm be, if in fact it ever existed? At least 100 years. I'd have to count on miraculous chance to find it, but what if I did? Would I feel the familiar churning within as I gazed into cellar holes, at moldered remnants of a root cellar (or "dairy," as was said), or mysterious metal gizmos whose functions within larger mystery devices would keep me speculating for long minutes and even for hours, if I had any hours left to me?

The answer: Yes, I believe.

The first part of the trek would take me through known country, full of all kinds of associations and memories by now—I've rambled here, and on similar ground, that long. At the end of the timber road we added to the territory a decade ago, I'd break into popple thicket, the trees too big to make grouse or woodcock cover anymore, but full of turkey tracks in all the seasons. There's a spring nearby, for larvae and grubs when other ground is frozen and snowed over, and a good stand of white oak too; our property lies almost at the very upper tip of the white oak's range, which I've always considered one more cause for celebration.

One August, bushwhacking through that popple tangle, I looked ahead and saw a hen turkey, and then her whole clutch of half-grown poults, a dozen plus, about chicken size, late brood. The adult bird was still protective: she'd run back and forth, trying to distract my attention; or she'd rush in close to shoo one of the young out of my presence; or she'd make herself big and try to stare me down.

I remember wondering how on earth I could ever have killed so vivid a creature, whose bravery and skill moved me so greatly that day. And she was physically beautiful too: below the ungainly head and neck, there's no better dressed fowl than the wild turkey, hen or tom. The sunshine filtered through the frail ceiling of aspen, and as it struck her feathers it mutely exploded in lights: I'd known of the browns and grays and beiges, but here there were golds and maroons and purples and magentas, along with other colors I could hardly believe existed in nature, or anywhere.

Valor and beauty in a so-called dumb beast: how could I contemplate doing her harm? I didn't resolve the question that summer morning, and won't now. Even as I marveled, though, I knew I'd get over my reservations. I knew I'd hunch in a blind, come May, knew I'd blow or scratch my call and feel my neck hairs itch to hear a gobbled answer. Conversing with a long-beard tom: that's part of another set of marvels—the almost preternatural keenness of his eyesight, his craftiness and caution, the war in his ample and oh-so-edible breast between an urge to propagate and one to survive. And there I've been and will be, to watch the war kindle.

Leaving the popple dungeon, I'd soon come to a brook, cross it, then shamble into young pine forest, where one spring I flushed a hen mallard, nested at least a half-mile from water of any kind. Belle had pointed her on her eggs, and, when the duck clattered off through the understorey, the dog looked as puzzled and surprised as I was.

No one, wild or human, could have predicted this turn of events, as I'm pleased to report.

Another half-mile beyond that out-of-the-way nesting ground, I'd arrive at another brook, which drops to The Connecticut, river of my heart, where all brooks in this part of the state must end. I'd crossed it before at a natural ford about a mile and a half east of its origin, but, having never traced it all the way to the valley, I wasn't sure where it traveled downstream from there (*though I will be sure soon, I resolve with satisfaction, when I ramble home territory again*).

I'd pause at the ford, all spangled granite and pebble just under the surface, a place where the wild iris are always profuse in mudtime, and the trillium so plentiful you can catch their soggy-animal smell ("Stinking Benjamin") a football field away on the right breeze.

Wild flowers, wild grounds.

Bellagio: an interlude

Tame flowers, tame grounds.

Sixteen years ago, in 1985, I was a fellow at the Villa Serbelloni in Bellagio, a comely, gold and pink town on the peninsula between the two arms of Lake Como. The villa was once the property of the Principe della Torre e Tasso. (In his other great house, near Trieste, Rainer Maria Rilke wrote *The Duino Elegies*). The Rockefeller Foundation runs the place now as a retreat for scholars and artists.

Never have poets or scholars been so splendidly catered to as we were in February of that year: I had my own little study in the woods, an ancient chapel still possessed, I felt sure, of something more than its own brick, wood and stucco; the meals and accommodations were nonpareil, the company stimulating and sympathetic. I got a great deal of writing done.

Or, more accurately, a lot of revision: for some reason it seemed beyond me to generate original work there, in spite of all those amenities.

Or maybe because of them. My failure of what's too cavalierly called inspiration had something to do, I now think, with an odd feeling of disembodiment: never a dish to wash, never a child to scold or comfort or dress or feed or even talk with; no wife, first reader and critic; no telephone; no unexpected visits from neighbors.

Yes, I could look back on work already accomplished, maybe with just the disinterested eye I needed, and maybe couldn't have applied otherwise.

But the new material wouldn't come.

The director of the Villa Serbelloni was the wonderfully humane Roberto Celli, who has died of cancer since then, and whom I and many others continue to mourn. Back then, at his suggestion, I took a few days off in the middle of my stay to visit a peasant family we'd befriended on our honeymoon in Umbria.

The immersion in day-to-day domesticity at the Doddis' seemed a perfect antidote to a mild depression I don't think I even knew I'd been suffering. It felt bracing just to lend a hand with the fire and to help in the kitchen, to be in the presence of the very young, to converse in a serious but not a so-called learned way with my hosts Franco and Rita.

The fire was always kindled, but kept low. Even though the house, ancient, was so low that I ducked through each doorway, there was a February chill in the place, which seemed somehow bracing after the perfect comfort of my room at Bellagio, a room the size of our living room at home. The scent of spice and olive oil reached to bed and bath; none of the utter quiet of solitude, either, that I knew in my little chapel study—rather, the endless mix of murmur and animation among the Doddi kin.

We all teased Serena, 14, about her boyfriend Ugo. We enounced that name in as ugly a way as possible. She blushed red as the coals, and cuffed us all in turn. Franco's goats rustled in the stable below, and the cocker Serafina, the mushroom hunter, snored by the hearth.

And yet after the Umbrian sojourn, I was still fated back at Bellagio to revision alone—not that the process proved any less pleasant than usual; and I needed to go through that process anyway, in order to make my third book of poems a good one, or as good as possible anyhow.

Make no mistake: I like to revise. I love it in fact, almost as much as composition itself. To revise means, literally, to see again, so that for me to wander back through my own strophes at the Villa Serbelloni was also to get a picture of a landscape. Not an Umbrian or Lombardian one, though; rather the one that waited for me at home, the rambler's ground.

That was a solace, because I could no more ramble in the Bellagian part of Italy than I've rambled in this part of Switzerland, for reasons I hope I've indicated. Not that I was merely sedentary. Every afternoon, in fair weather and otherwise, I'd take a ferry across the Como arm of the lake. I can still see the surface fracted into diamonds, hear the throb of the diesel under the Latin palaver of fellow passengers, feel that same throb under my boot soles. Debarking, I'd stop for a small coffee, neat, at the post office *café,* and chat with its owner—a rotund and cheery fellow whose face God had copied from Currier and Ives renditions of Santa Claus. Then I'd climb one of four pre-Alpine mountains behind the village of Menaggio.

I could see the Dolomites from any peak, the whole tooth shape of the lake, the magnificent villas on both the east and west shores. After flogging my bulk up all that steepness, following or crossing ancient mule trails, passing flower-decked shrines to the virgin at every bridge or ford over the frigid *torrente*, at land's height I could marvel at farmhouses and barns, complete with tessellated orange roofs and well pruned olives: these were summer redoubts, where herdsmen drove their stock after snowmelt. I could imagine the perfume of jasmine and broom in May, the delicate blossoms on pear trees espaliered to their south-facing walls. The wet mud of the highlands made me think of mudtime in New England, a much reviled season, but one I cherish, everything breaking into *vita nuova.*

My sense of my heroism as a hiker was, needless to say, appropriately humbled by these farmsteads: civilization, even at these remote elevations!

Six weeks ago, I revisited Bellagio and the Villa Serbelloni with my family. Inglorious truth to tell, we were fleeing an infestation of head lice (*pidocchi*), which had plagued our Montagnola household for the better part of a month, off and on. Switzerland is the last place on earth you'd expect that problem, of course, and I'm more or less sure that the bugs hopped us while we rode the plane over. (Italian friends want to believe otherwise: they're delighted to think that the proper, spic-and-span Swiss, who so condescend to the Italians, and to outlanders in general, should be responsible for our fleas). Wherever they came from, the lice had proved incredibly resistant to treatment. We can laugh about them now, but we were all close to insanity then.

At one point I called a local dermatologist's office, having heard of an electric comb that—like some Gulf War "smart bomb"—would seek out the pests louse by louse and shock them dead. Speaking to the nurse, I asked her if she had ever heard of such a device. Yet I'd had a momentary lapse in vocabulary, couldn't recall the word *pettine,* "comb," and so, as I often do, I though of *peigne,* the French equivalent, and came up with *pigna,* which—as I well knew if I'd been thinking straight—means "pine cone."

She: "An electric *pine cone*?"

I: "Exactly, dear Madame."

She: "I'll ask *il dottore*."

The Villa Serbelloni's promontory was once the domain of the elder Pliny, who, for reasons that I pretentiously imagined I understood that day, named the hill *Tragoedia*. The prospects there of course prompted their share of emotions in me, including, however banally, a certain melancholy. I'd been 42 in 1985; I thought I knew something then about time's flight.

And I did. I simply didn't know as much as I do now, my beloved mother, for one example among too many others, dead in the interval between the time of the Vermont rambles I've recorded and our arrival here in Europe.

My mother and I—as I've said elsewhere, that's the stuff of at least another full book. I do know at least that part of what I pondered at Tragoedia was how proud she'd been, a decade and a half back, of my invitation to stay there, where my institutional hosts were the exalted Rockefellers, where I'd be hobnobbing with people of real eminence. The whole thing made me proud for her sake too: I was showing her at last that her firstborn might be a grownup, even if he had his own private doubts about such a matter.

Come back! I inwardly whimper now and then, in the manner of all orphans over the eons.

Yes, there was melancholy at Bellagio in 2001, but also a certain tension in my soul, even though it wasn't blooming season for anything, as I contemplated the beauty and scrupulousness of the Villa's gardens, the splendor of the buildings. I felt it too as we explored the town's slim streets, along which we found houses that had offered temporary but productive haven, for example, to Stendhal.

At one point, in fact, while I stopped to read a plaque dedicated to Franz Liszt, who'd composed his sonata "after reading Dante" in one of these very houses, I caught myself imagining a small apartment in the neighborhood. I'd still rather eat glass than set myself up in Mad River Glen, Stowe, Stratton, above all odious, omnivorous Killington in Vermont. But I could somehow picture living with the well considered "development" that's been underway on these hills and by these shores since the time of Pliny himself and even before.

In short, and alarmingly, I was flirting with the *bourgeois* devotion to "civilization," more especially to its creature comforts, and above all to its monuments, no matter that these—in the acute judgment of a Walter Benjamin—are inevitably monuments as well to barbarism: plunder, exploitation, naked power unleashed.

But politics weren't uppermost in my thoughts, I admit. As I imagined that apartment, the morning's *macchiato* at lakeside while I lingered over the rose-colored *Gazzetta dello Sport* or over *La Repubblica*, I was also wondering whether I could still climb Monte Tremezzo as quickly as I did in my fellowship days—and more importantly, whether I would. If not, was that just in the nature of the "civilized" fantasy? Or did it rather cause the fantasy?

In whichever case, both in 1985 and a decade and a half later I knew that those climbs, plenty strenuous enough, were never really rambles. That made for one of my skepticisms about the civilized Bellagio apartment. Yet my daydream, however momentary, left me wondering what I'd come to, physically and otherwise. A nice little retreat on Como's shores? I was playing with fire: time to get back to writing about rambles, at least, if I couldn't take one.

It was *time.*

It is time.

Day two (reprise)

I WOULD STOP FOR A SPELL AT MY TREASURED FORD, WHERE I'D COCK MY ears to the flutey run of clear water over the stone bar.

I say all this on la Collina d'oro, the hill of gold, as the Ticinesi call our neighborhood, where it doesn't matter right now—in fact it may help—that my ears are congenitally poor, and worsened by however many muzzle-blasts they've suffered: I hear that Yankee brook.

I can almost taste it too, wild and cold.

With cupped palms, I'd take in draft after draft from the frothed eddy that whirls under the south cutbank. The best drink God ever made. ("Adam's Ale," some call it.) Then northward again.

No trick for me to ransack the mind's store, to drink from a hundred similar brooks. My memory's crammed with rambles, with sensory knowledge, and maybe other kinds, of what might lie up that way beyond the ford: perhaps another rotting lumber ramp or two; slats from someone's long-tumbled horse hovel; asters along the margins of a burntland now coming back to woods; some early autumn smell, a harbinger of the earth gone tight with ice; the yawning croak of a raven or the cartoon laughter of a pileated; the husked-up fruit on a butternut tree, which, like the rest of its kind, now gives itself up to an ugly blight, triangular galls like vandals' etchings on the rough trunk: goodbye, old pasture and cabinet tree, old dropper of nuts for kids to throw at each other in mock battle; a vacant fox den; a deer; a moose; a vole, mouse, or muskrat; a comic porcupine daring me to catch up, waddling ahead on a game-trace, devil-may-care.

I could even string the observations I'd imagine from that second day into some semblance of narrative coherence, because it all—everything—does come together somewhere: bird and beast and cloud and Tink-Dolly-Ray-Creston-Zane-Allie-Dave and my good dog Belle and my wife and five children and even this far Ticino; that late cab and the marble effigy of Pliny the elder at Tragoedia and snow on our backyard palms and the camellias and daffodils on the hillsides and the railroad sleepers hewn by Uncle George and my mother and father and my late brother and living siblings and my friends Joey and Nancy and Don and Steve and Peter and Tommy and Landy and Bruce and Leslie and Paul and Ruth and Marv and Louise and on and on.

But to offer such an account, after all, even if it wouldn't quite be fictive, to play at such seamlessness: no matter Imagination's "awful power," that would be to ramble without truly rambling, to write another sort of testimony.

So I'm about done for a spell.

No more reprise for now, to recall a word I've used and re-used in my reveries here. The word suggests a "taking again," and if I leave off my own reprises for a while, it's with the rambler's hope that I can indeed take (or be taken) again, and repeatedly: although we depart on our wanderings as unpremeditatedly as we can, meditation does catch up with us, and although in temporary conclusion we always wend our ways home, we pray to such higher powers as we envision that we'll do so for as close to forever as possible.

Maybe forever, pure and simple.

This morning, March 14, 2001, came on wondrously bright in the Ticino. I took time to enjoy a hike. Well, no; it was no more, really, than a walk. Perhaps counting on sympathetic imagination, however, I'd put on the battered clothes I wear on my Vermont rambles, ones I wear and wear and wear till they're worn out—then on to the next small epoch of denim and flannel and leather and woods and contemplation.

As I passed the house where Hermann Hesse wrote all these years ago, I felt an itch about halfway up my calf on the bad-hip side. By the side of the path, I saw a convenient bench (the Swiss are so civilized!), sat, and rolled back the trouser leg. There on its inside seam I saw nothing less than a single beggar tick, a last clinger from the Friday rambles

I've chronicled, a laundry survivor. (It had to be: the burr doesn't exist here, and these are the only pants I wore over those two days.)

At that instant, the physical itch turned into the other kind. I'd cursed the beggar ticks collectively seven months ago, all right; but today I found myself muttering strange blessings on this solitary. It was, after all, a token of the little wildness I treasure, and, as I held it between thumb and finger, its tiny presence suddenly transformed the spectacular Ticinese landscape. Far mountains shrank into lower, more beckoning hills; even the flowering trees and shrubs in the near distance, as in some *trompe l'oeil* painterly effect became serviceberry, hawthorn, black cherry, early apple.

A small corner of New England, with all its variety, color and thicketiness, flashed upon the inward eye, as Wordsworth once famously called it. The reprise of a burr became a grander reprise.

Maybe—I hope so, religiously—there will always be some itch to set me going, to draw me into the rambler's landscape, to write of that as I may.

On that second day, as on any day, I suspect I'd have prayed. For what? What else? A little wildness forever. Out there and—despite time's hurry—within.

December, 2000–April, 2001
Montagnola